The Art of Papercutting

Jessica Palmer

SEARCH PRESS

First published in Great Britain 2015

Search Press Limited
Wellwood, North Farm Road,
Tunbridge Wells, Kent TN2 3DR

Text copyright © Jessica Palmer 2015

Studio photographs by Paul Bricknell at Search Press Studios,
other photographs the author's own unless specified
Studio photographs and design copyright © Search Press
Ltd. 2015

ISBN 978 1 78221 066 5

The Publishers and author can accept no responsibility for
any consequences arising from the information, advice or
instructions given in this publication.

Suppliers

If you have any difficulty obtaining any of the materials
and equipment mentioned in this book, please visit the
Search Press website: **www.searchpress.com**

Publisher's note: All photographs of papercutting workshops
are the author's own. Where the papercuts shown are by
students, every effort has been made to gain permission and
acknowledge the artist.

Author's note: To anyone I have not been able to reach,
I would like to convey my sincere thanks and appreciation.
Thanks go to all the students I have worked with who have
helped me learn so much about the art of papercutting.

You are invited to visit the author's website:
www.jessicapalmerart.com

Printed in China

Front cover:
Illustrating Life With a Knife
*This is my homage to Danish illustrator, Kay Nielsen. It is
a digitally coloured papercut.*

Page 1:
Jane's Garden
This papercut also appears on page 70.

Page 3:
Edo Reflection
This papercut has been digitally coloured.

The Art of
Papercutting

Dedication

I would like to dedicate this book to my husband, Keith, for his indefatigable wit and his intelligence; to my daughter, Katie, for her inspiration and beauty; to my son, Ben, for his calming presence and to my friend, Cath Howe, for her incisive mind and generosity of spirit.

Contents

INTRODUCTION

I have called this book *The Art of Papercutting* because papercutting gives me endless artistic possibilities. Papercutting is often thought of as a craft because it has its roots in a craft tradition of skill and repetition. But for me it is the unpredictability of this medium that I love. In a world where it is possible to create anything digitally, a hand-cut picture has the unique appeal of any handmade object, with its character and imperfections. And though I use a digital drawing tablet in my illustration work, I usually draw the first sketch of any piece with a knife, before scanning and colouring it digitally on the computer. This early cutting out process stretches my mind and helps me come up with an original approach.

I found my way to papercutting during an MA in Illustration, carried out over two years of juggling childcare and artwork. During that time, I experimented with every medium under the sun. Then one day, in a life drawing class, an innovative tutor took the charcoal out of my hand, gave me a pair of scissors and said, 'Cut it out!' My early cuts vaguely resembled Matisse-style images: large, boldly drawn figures using whatever colour paper I could get my hands on. From there I graduated swiftly from scissors to a knife.

There was something infinitely satisfying about freehand cutting with a scalpel blade. Cutting out helped my drawing. Instead of producing a dithery line, I started to draw confidently, and in a way that was recognisably my own style. I brought collage and cut images into each project I tackled. Drawing with a knife was a linear process: a study of the contour or the outline of an object. Gradually, as I embarked on my self-taught 10,000-hour drawing apprenticeship, I began to see how with light, shadow, layering, texture and infinite pattern, it was possible to make paper work with as much range and depth as any other medium.

As is visible in Matisse's paper cut-outs, a papercutter's medium is not the knife or the scissors they use, but the paper. Matisse's palette of paper was coloured to a carefully calibrated range by his assistants. It was inspired by the hues and light of southern France, making the work identifiably his.

The human eye also loves monochrome, and another reason for the popularity of the papercut image is the appeal of the simplicity of black on white, as well as the silhouetted shape on a contrasting background.

The qualities of paper – its texture, transparency, reflective aspects, weight and resilience – give the papercutter a wide set of opportunities. A papercutter can use practically any paper available. The trick is to find the type of paper to match the end product. I have made pieces with newsprint, 1950s food magazines, Indian silk paper, synthetic paper, Offenbach Bible paper, photocopy paper, Japanese washi paper, 1930s newsletters about magic tricks and crumpled gold paper from an art store in New York. My overflowing plan chest is evidence of my love of paper and magpie-like obsession with collecting it.

In any artwork, it is usually the thinking and planning that takes the longest time. For me, this can take several weeks as I work out a picture until I can see it in my mind's eye. I think about the drawing, deciding on negative and positive areas of the image, and about how to use pattern, proportion, and the relationship and connectivity of shapes as well as the balance of cut and uncut paper in the whole piece.

As I am an illustrator by training, my instinct is to make a story-telling image with movement and figurative depictions. I approach this in combination with the particular features of papercutting, such as linking, flowing one part into another, using borders, or stylising a face to make the image into a striking design.

My technique is to combine the traditions of silhouetted images with extra line, pattern and emphasis. I use the point of my scalpel blade like the tip of a pencil. My pieces are made up of sequences of patterns – sometimes observed, sometimes invented. These shape my images and give them depth, shine, personality or humour. In this book, I hope to share with you my passion for paper and some of my techniques for transforming this humble yet phenomenally diverse material into fantastical works of art.

Opposite

The Pleasure Garden. This piece is 1 metre x 80cm (1 yard x 31½in), and was cut from one sheet of paper. Author's own photograph.

The story of papercutting

Papercutting probably began as a courtly pastime, but it gradually became widely practised as a folk art in many parts of the world. The Chinese invented paper around 105 AD and papercutting was an inexpensive alternative to using paints, brushes and canvases. The tradition extended across the world from China to Japan, India, Mexico and eventually central Europe. People cut stencils for wall or window decoration or made papercuts for ornaments, good luck charms or embroidery patterns. Papercut designs are a feature of celebrations and festivals such as the Day of the Dead in Mexico, where the paper *picado* or papercut banner is punched with a hammer, chiselled, gouged and pierced to create long chains of images.

Papercutting became popular in England during the 18th and 19th centuries. The most familiar approach to cutting paper is silhouetting, which was a cheaper alternative to painted portraits. Travelling papercutters would go from village to village, cutting likenesses of families but also of trees, flowers, birds and animals. There is an early example of a papercut called 'Bear in a Landscape', dating from about 1709 by Mary West in the Holburne Museum in Bath.

Another way of working with cut paper, which started around this time, was what we would now call a collage. One of the best practitioners of this form was Mary Delany (1700–1788) who cut tiny pieces of hand-painted paper to create her beautiful 'paper mosaiks' of botanically accurate plants and flowers. A collection of these collages is in the British Museum in London. Mary Delany embarked on this cut paper technique when she was seventy-two and only gave up when she lost her sight in her eighties. An heroically late starter and an example to all snippers and cutters!

Asphodil Lily
This papercut of mine, cut from magazine pages, is an homage to the work of Mary Delany. Author's own photograph.

This Polish style piece, or wycinanki, is cut from many coloured papers superimposed on a black paper layer to make an outline. It is a symmetrical piece, cut by folding the paper in half and then drawing the design onto the folded side of the paper. Typically of folk art, it makes maximum use of minimal materials for decorative effect. Author's own photograph.

This heart was cut from purple origami paper for a workshop called 'A Knife to the Heart' at the Victoria & Albert Museum. Author's own photograph.

Early papercutters used all kinds of tools. Some used large, oval-handled scissors with short, sharp blades. Others used chisels, stamps and punches, and even sheep shears.

In China, where paper was invented, papercutting is known as *jian shi*. In Japan it is known as *kirigami*. *Kirigami* involves folding the paper then cutting. In the example above, the heart was folded from purple origami paper and then cut from the centre fold with scissors.

Lunar Sheep

Contemporary Chinese papercuts are often based on ancient patterns. They are usually cut on flat rather than folded paper, and often from a bold colour like red. Traditional Chinese symbols and figures are as old as papercutting itself and include fish, flowers, lanterns, dragons, birds and images from folk tales or the Chinese zodiac. This image was cut in a very simple and traditional Chinese style to promote events at the Museum of East Asian Art in Bath and to commemorate the Lunar Year of the Sheep. Author's own photograph. A template for this papercut is provided on page 133.

Seeing as a papercutter

Before you begin any papercut piece, you need to start to see the image with the eyes of a papercutter. This is the bit that provides great exercise for the brain. It is often the moment in my workshops when people look a bit dazed and confused – but stay with me for a moment. It is simpler than you think. You need to break any image down into positive and negative areas and shapes. If you are working with black paper, which you will mount on a white background, the black is the positive and the white is the negative. The negative is the part you cut away. The positive is the part you leave behind which becomes your papercut drawing.

I often think that papercutting is more similar to carving stone or wood than applying paint because the process is one of whittling away until you achieve the image you want. What makes this tricky is that our eyes see many gradations of colour and tone, so to convert a drawing, painting or photograph into a papercut means not just simplifying it into two tones but redesigning the image so that it sits comfortably in two dimensions.

Seeing positive and negative shapes

Filigree Paper

In these two images, you can see that the positive section has been removed from the left-hand papercut and placed on its own, making two very beautiful shapes from one morsel of paper. Author's own photographs.

 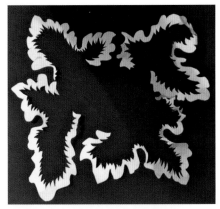

Roar

These two images of a lion, by a student at the Victoria & Albert Museum, were cut from a single piece of paper. As she cut the negative lion (above, she placed all the pieces she removed next to it to create a positive lion at the same time (right). This takes time and concentration but I have included it here to show the distinct difference in effect of a positive papercut drawing and a negative one. Author's own photograph.

Thinking about the design

In the picture opposite, 'Lets Talk About Love', I began with the idea of a story in a peacock's tail. I wanted to use the alternate negative and positive cut faces to show various faces in black and white. I planned my drawing, marking up the negative portions I would then cut away.

You will also want to choose which way the image is facing. In some images it is not important. In others, particularly those involving faces or depictions of actual places, it is crucial to ensure that you cut the image in reverse so that it comes out the right way round. There is a simple way to do this on page 48.

A key consideration is always to decide in advance if you want your papercut to be in a border or frame. In this image, I wanted a frame and chose to make this up of feather shapes that seemed an extension of the peacock's tail, encompassing the whole. It is usually worth designing a border at the beginning. You can cut it away later if you prefer.

To extend the whimsical feel of this piece, I mounted it on patterned white silk paper. For more about mounting papercuts, take a look at pages 34 and 35.

Success in papercutting is a matter of planning and doing a good drawing in advance. I have found that, as with many activities in life, the more thinking and envisaging you can do in advance, the better the eventual outcome will be. A strong drawing will give you a head start. After 10,000 hours of papercutting (which roughly equates to working every day for five years), I do sometimes cut out freehand, but I am invariably happier with those pieces I have let simmer in my mind for a while.

In this 'Blue Bird Dress', the fun challenge I gave myself was to construct the shape of the dress purely from the outlines of birds. I also wanted to inject humour and a sense of a story or conversation between the birds. You will have noticed that birds are a recurrent theme in my work. I love their silhouettes, expressive movement and feathers, and their infinite variety.

Opposite
Let's Talk About Love
Author's own photograph.

Blue Bird Dress
I painted the paper for this piece myself because I like the variation in intensity of colour that you get with hand-painted paper. Author's own photograph.

Making everything join together

As Oscar Wilde said, 'One should either be a piece of art or wear a piece of art'! These images show some of my wearable paper art – kindly modelled by my daughter, Katie. This concept originally came about because I was playing with the idea of connected imagery and wanted to see how far I could take it. You do not have to make everything link up in a papercut – it can be made up of any number of separate sections. However, there is something satisfying in making an image in which everything is interconnected. It makes you think hard about the design and the layout of the image, and if you are making a three-dimensional or freestanding piece like this necklace, it is obviously essential.

Black Bird Necklace

This was designed as part of an illustration for a book. But then I realised it would make a spectacular collar. I used a synthetic paper so that it would not tear on its first outing. There is more about paper on pages 32–33. Author's own photograph.

Flower Collar

This was made for a springtime party on a floral theme, to be worn draped over a white dress. Note the contrasting positive (black) and negative (white) flowers. The grid pattern holds the design elements together and has a lacy quality. Author's own photograph.

Mexico Meets France Necklace

This was made for a friend, Jane Sigal's engagement party, and it was an excellent conversational icebreaker! The brief was to combine French elements, including a Napoleonic eagle and honey bees, with Mexican references, some of which I sourced from an ancient mural of birds and flowers. The challenge was to join these into a shape that could be worn, and would work with Jane's Mexican wedding dress. The colour was chosen to match the simple pink embroidery on the dress. Author's own photograph.

Ladies in Hats

This piece was inspired by a celebration of Georgian art and style. This was a bit of fun for me in preparation for a workshop about paper necklaces. I am particularly fond of silhouettes and the idea that there is a conversation going on between the characters in the piece. The paper is hand-sprayed in a deliberately uneven way for texture and interest. As with the Mexico Meets French Necklace, the linking elements are leaves and flowers. It might look scratchy but it is surprisingly comfortable, light and easy to wear. Author's own photograph.

17

Looking at nature

Nature supplies me with all kinds of decorative ideas when I am planning a papercut design. I look at the ridges on a shell, the skeletal fragment of a leaf, the intricacy of a pine cone or the silhouette of a seed head. Each of these can give a rhythm to a design or a suggestion for an arrangement of shapes. Sometimes a papercutting workshop will be arranged around a nature theme. This was the case with 'Papercutting the Power of the Sea' at the Royal West of England Academy in Bristol. Laura Murray was one of the students there.

Laura arrived with a black and white photocopy of an impressionistic painting of the sea. It was an unlikely choice, being far from the graphic and linear style of image that I would normally recommend as a starting point for papercutting. Laura chose blue coated paper and used carbon paper to transfer her drawing onto her paper (see pages 46–47). She did a lot of squinting at the original painting and managed to sort out the swirls of grey and black into a graphic pattern of repeating shapes. She knew she wanted her positive area – the blue – to represent the water, and the white – or cutaway negative area – to be the foamy crests of the waves.

The result is a crisp, dynamic image which captures all the movement and ferocity of the original waves but is a completely distinct work of art.

Note

Scattered through this book, you will find examples of wonderful work made by participants in my paper art workshops. I deliver occasional workshops in museums and galleries. The environments and the students provide me with inspiration and an opportunity to learn as much as to teach.

Laura Murray at work during my sea-themed workshop. Author's own photograph.

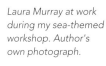

Waves
A workshop piece by Laura Murray. Photograph courtesy of Laura Murray.

How to create tone and texture

For this image of King Charles I of England, based on a portrait in the Dulwich Picture Gallery, the main decorative element was to be the texture of the lace collar. Using the technique of breaking down the image into positive and negative space, I chose to represent the lace through a series of vertical bars, angled at one end. These are edged by around twelve tiny diamond cuts at the base of each bar, to give an impression of a protruding ruff. This is a simplification of the actual painted look of the lace. This act of simplifying is part of the process of arriving at a pleasing papercut design.

Charles I is young in this image, so I have cut wiggly curves in his hair to represent his luscious, wavy locks. The slashes in his sleeves, showing off his expensive white undershirt, are crimped and wide open to convey a sense of the generosity of his garments.

Charles I
Author's own photograph.

And Then...

This is one of a sequence of illustrations for a story about a princess. I used many random patterns for the cakes, strawberries and pineapple, to contrast with the geometric, repeating patterns in the ballgown. The large area of positive or black gives a sense of solidity for the table. The stylised birds on the fabric of the dress contrast with the naturalistic feather fan the princess holds in her left hand. You can see how papercutting – as a linear form of drawing – is good for creating a sense of soft, fleshy curves as well as for the billowing folds of the character's shawl. Author's own photograph.

Pattern — the papercutter's key to success

I begin any papercut with a pencil drawing. Here I start to map out areas that are positive and negative. I draw in as much detail as I can in advance, in the sure knowledge that this will change and evolve in the final papercut.

At this stage, I think about pattern within the papercut. This pattern is my light and dark, texture and contour, tone and decoration. I look for ideas about pattern in everything around me from lace to armour, from insects to trees. This is really an extension of the idea of breaking an image down into positive and negative areas. The next stage is to think about the shapes you will cut out. These may be geometric or organic. They may be repeated or scattered unevenly. The three examples shown here are by students in my workshops.

I tend to think in terms of either a formal or informal pattern. The pattern shown below, left, is sourced from a plaster architectural detail, and is quite formal. The shapes are carefully designed and evenly spaced. The fossil on the right is more informal: the cutaway shapes have an uneven arrangement, and give us a clue about the shadowed bumps and edges.

The most successful papercuts are achieved where areas of pattern are balanced with solid areas left uncut.

A student in one of my workshops working on a formal pattern. Author's own photograph.

A more natural, less formal pattern, again from a workshop. Author's own photograph.

A student at a Tudor Art workshop at the Holburne Museum in Bath was inspired by embroidery on a Tudor painting to cut this delicate curlicue. Author's own photograph.

Finding inspiration

As I begin to plan a papercut and think about cutting dots, loops, scoops, squares, diamonds, tears, triangles, slivers, moons and curls, I look around for sources of imagery. I get inspiration from looking at the world around me. It sounds an obvious thing to say, but the fundamental aspect of my development as an artist has been learning to observe objects, faces, locations and so on. Observation is clearly a key to drawing confidently, and it can also provide you with a way to organise a picture. An excellent way to start a papercut is with a simple line drawing that you embellish as you cut.

For a Valentine's Day card, I noticed this simple engraving on a silver box. I simplified it and added the birds and words. I was trying to retain the handmade simplicity of the image. I then mounted it on pink paper. Author's own photographs.

A good way to start any papercut is to think about whether the image is going to sit within a frame or border. I often look at stained glass and other windows for inspiring arrangements of space. Author's own photograph.

Tiger Lady
This image contains a combination of things I like and patterns I love: dragonflies' glassy wings, repeated geometric shapes, tiger stripes, organic leaves twining around the figure, a bird and feather shapes, fabric in folds and the silhouette of a damsel in some disarray. When it was completed, I scanned this black and white papercut and coloured it digitally for publication. You can colour in a paper cut in many different ways. Here I was trying to capture the soft luminosity of stained glass. Author's own photograph.

I was commissioned to do a life-story portrait which needed to include many different elements including Sherlock Holmes and the Beatles. I happened to be walking past St Martin-in-the-Fields Church in London and saw this window (right). It gave me a structure for the papercut in which to place all the themes of the portrait (far right). The portrait is shown larger on page 62. Author's own photographs.

One aspect of papercutting that can make for striking graphic images is simplification. Working with a scalpel, however sharp, will generally mean that some details will be lost. I try to turn this into a design virtue. By looking at a complex shape like the head of this wild angelica flower (below), and simplifying it into tiny fingers of paper, you can achieve an impression of floral texture and capture the overall character of the plant, if not the botanical detail (below, right). A student at Shepherds Bookbinders cut this out of blue paper, then chose to mount it on gold paper for a dramatic contrast. For more about mounting papercuts, see pages 34–37. Author's own photographs.

Seed Head
Author's own photograph. The template is provided on page 138.

As many people who have done a workshop with me will know, I will often hand out a small drawing of an iris for their first papercut. This is to give students a chance to familiarise themselves with the feel of the knife, mat and paper, as well as to learn the best position for their hands and fingers. It is also because an iris is a set of fluid shapes with few angles or straight lines. The loops, curls and whorls of the plant's shape are a good place to begin to learn the art of cutting out. What is astonishing is the way in which students interpret my replica drawing in a variety of unique ways – some silhouetting, some outlining, some framing, some adding pattern and some mounting their cut in a novel way, as in this example. Author's own photographs.

Getting Started

Materials

Papercutting is a low-budget pursuit. All you really need to get started is a pencil, a knife, a cutting mat and some paper. Here are a few pointers.

Basic equipment

Scalpel I strongly recommend a size 5 Swan Morton scalpel handle with interchangeable blades – either 10, 10a or 11 – whichever you prefer. These are the scalpels used in medical practice and I find them easier to use and more precise than the usual craft knives. Papercutting is a way of drawing, and these knives are the closest to the shape and weight of a pencil or pen. Change the blade regularly. You know when the tip is blunt if you gently drag it along the paper and it does not cut through. Use **jewellery pliers** to remove blades (see page 42). Wrap a strip of **bookbinder's** or **masking tape** around the scalpel blade where it fits onto the handle to protect your fingertips and make it more comfortable.

Self-healing cutting mat This is very important for safety and accuracy. Do not try to cut on cardboard, glass or wood. In papercutting, the knife needs to make contact with the mat, and in a self-healing mat, that cut then closes, leaving you a smooth surface on which to make the next cut. Keep your mat flat and don't glue on it or rest your coffee on it. Self-healing cutting mats buckle in heat or moisture and if left standing on their edge. They come in a wide range of sizes. An A3 mat is a good size to start with.

Low-tack sticky tape This is very handy for repairs to your papercuts. Keep a strip of tape on the mat and stick small sections over any part you want to repair. Stick repairs to the back of the papercut so that when you turn it over, they are invisible.

Carbon and tracing papers I always encourage my students to draw freehand. However, where you want to transfer a drawing or any image to the paper you are going to cut, carbon paper is a useful way to do this quickly and simply. For an explanation about how to do this, see page 46.

Pencils Keep a variety to hand: hard pencils for transferring images, softer pencils for freehand drawing.

Glue pens These are very useful for sticking down small papercuts by dabbing glue in strategic places.

Metal ruler This is good to have for cutting the straight edges of borders.

Hole punch These can be useful for repeating patterns, though I use them very rarely.

Opposite:
Clockwise from top left: low-tack sticky tape, masking tape, carbon paper, tracing paper, magnifiying glass, glue pen, bookbinder's tape, hole punch, cutting mat, scalpel and blades, paper clips, ruler, pencils, nail scissors, pencil sharpener, compasses, jewellery pliers and eraser.

Magnifying glass When doing detailed papercuts, even the youngest eyes can benefit from using a magnifying glass clipped to the table over your work. Make sure you work in good light too, with a **daylight bulb** in your **lamp** for evenings.

Paper clips These are handy for keeping layers of paper together when you are transferring images.

Nail scissors These are usually the best for any kind of folded papercutting. Find the sharpest pair you can with the most pointed tips.

Compasses Handy for curving lines and circles in papercut drawings.

Paper — the papercutter's palette

As a papercutter, the paper you use provides your palette of colour, texture, depth and even quality of line as you cut. It sometimes seems that there are as many different types of paper as there are people. I am a paper magpie and collect it wherever I see it. I have a large plan chest that contains papers for cutting, mounting, modeling into paper sculpture, collage, papier-mâché, folding, crumpling and curling. These may be silk papers, synthetic papers, recycled papers, old paper from vintage books or magazines, wrapping paper, bookbinding paper, origami paper, newspaper or lace paper… The list goes on.

Practically any type of paper can be cut. However, the lighter weight papers that are 40, 50 or 60gsm (photocopy paper is around 80gsm just to give you an approximate idea) are the best and easiest to cut. The first paper I cut out was a page from an old book. It was very thick. It blunted my knife and hurt my fingers, and it was difficult to get a clean line.

I now work with 50gsm white paper which I buy from a specialist paper supplier. It has a smooth surface and can be hand coloured with paint or ink without it bleeding through to the other side. This means that one side of the paper stays white so you can draw on it.

I sometimes want the variation of colour that comes from hand painting. If I am looking for a flatter surface, I use coated paper, which is printed with a colour on one side and white on the other. This comes in a huge range of colours and sizes, and can have a matt, silky or metallic finish.

In a papercutting workshop, first timers usually start with matt black coated paper in either A4 or A3 size. This is a good way to begin as working in black and white helps them to learn the process of thinking in positive and negative.

Materials for mounting and display

A papercut can be presented framed, unframed or loosely pinned to a wall in, for example, an exhibition. For regular presentation, and to preserve the papercut from dust or other damage, I usually use a box or deep frame, sometimes with a double mount, to allow the papercut to be raised above the surface of the mounting paper. To do this, I mount the papercut using small self-adhesive foam pads. See the opposite page for more about how to do this. Raising the papercut allows the viewer to recognise it as a papercut and to see the shadow it casts. If the papercut is pressed against glass, it can look like an ink drawing, and all your cutting efforts can go unseen.

If you don't want to use the foam pads and you are mounting a papercut directly onto card, paper or watercolour paper, use a glue pen to dab small dots of glue onto the back of the papercut.

I mount papercuts on a variety of surfaces depending on the subject, size and colour of the cut. Almost anything cut out of black looks best on a pure white background. However, I sometimes use translucent lace papers to add interest or another dimension. Watercolour paper can be an excellent mounting surface. Simple papercuts can be presented on richly patterned washi paper. White papercuts look good on patterned, coloured or black backgrounds.

I also like to experiment photographing my papercuts on crumpled paper, on layers of paper with light shining in between and with exaggerated shadow. See more about this on pages 118–125.

Using self-adhesive foam pads

You can buy the sticky pads at stationers' shops and they come in a variety of sizes. You can also cut them to fit if they are too large or the wrong shape.

1 In a delicate papercut like this leaf, find a few larger areas on which to stick the pads.

2 The pads will usually be repositionable so I suggest lightly placing the papercut, then lifting it if you are not happy with the position. Replace the papercut and gently press down on the areas where the pads are.

The pads are now invisible but you can clearly see the three-dimensional quality of the papercut.

Here you can see the eye-popping contrast of a white papercut on a black background (below, left), which strongly emphasises each cut line. The same papercut is shown (below, right) on a patterned paper surface that softens the image and makes it feel more organic and natural. The artichoke is cut from a pure white paper.

A double mount

The two layers of card ensure that, once framed, the edges of the papercut are lifted above the surface of the background paper.

Ash Tree

The tree, leaves and letters have a pleasing curl that enhances their leafiness. This is cut from hand-painted paper and mounted on oil painting paper which has a machine-textured canvas finish. The template for this papercut is provided on page 139.

Techniques

Cutting with a knife

I prefer to think of this as drawing with a knife. This is why it is important to hold the knife as you would any drawing tool. Try to work in a well-lit position, close to a window or using an anglepoise lamp with a daylight bulb. Ensure that you are sitting on a low chair or at a high table so that your back is not too curved over.

1 Most of the time you will be cutting – or drawing – with the tip of the knife, as you would with a sharp pencil. Make sure the knife sits comfortably in your hand. Hold it the way you would a pencil or a pen. Wrap masking tape or bookbinders' tape around the part of the scalpel handle where it joins the blade to protect your fingers and give you a better grip.

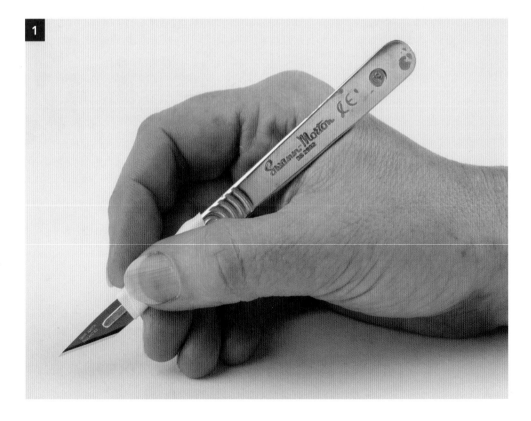

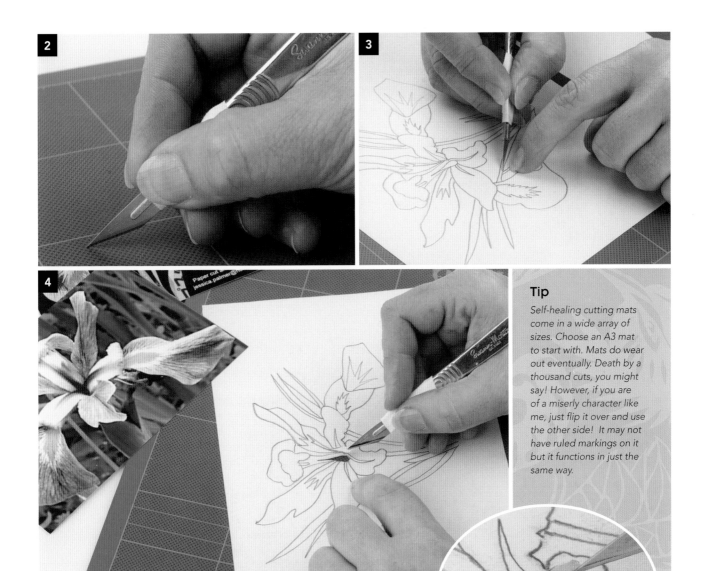

Tip

Self-healing cutting mats come in a wide array of sizes. Choose an A3 mat to start with. Mats do wear out eventually. Death by a thousand cuts, you might say! However, if you are of a miserly character like me, just flip it over and use the other side! It may not have ruled markings on it but it functions in just the same way.

2 Always use a self-healing cutting mat. It is important that the tip of the knife meets the surface of the mat as you cut. This is essential for your control of the knife blade and for safety. The mat will prevent your knife from slipping and the cuts you make in the mat will seal up, leaving a smooth surface on which to make further cuts.

3 Hold the knife firmly but without excessive pressure, keeping it at roughly a 45-degree angle to the paper. Use the forefinger of your opposite hand to guide the tip of the knife and to keep the paper from slipping or stretching. Keep your other fingers tucked in to protect them. Always cut towards yourself, as this will give you more control over the line you are cutting.

4 With your reference material close at hand, begin cutting from the centre of the image and work outwards gradually, turning the paper as necessary. Take small pieces at a time. Lift out the bits of paper you are removing with the tip of the scalpel blade.

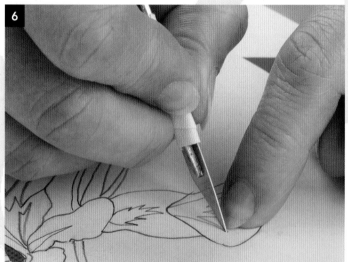

5 Use the straight edge of the scalpel blade to cut straight lines, holding the scalpel at a slightly lower angle to the paper.

6 Use the tip of the blade to cut sharp angles, digging the tip firmly into the mat and moving the paper to cut the opposite angle.

7 Cutting a circle is achieved by making a series of very short, straight cuts, moving the paper around and keeping the knife inserted into the paper. You might cut a circle of the size shown in eight to ten cuts.

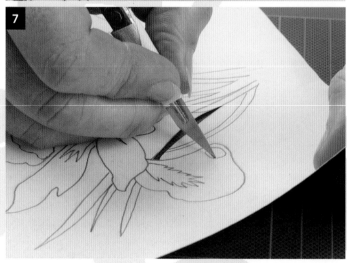

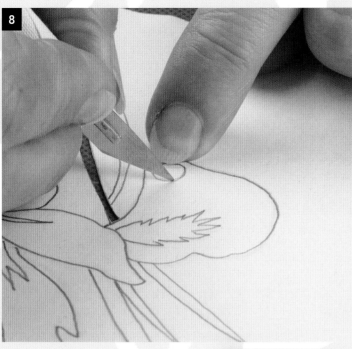

8 Make the first cut. Turn the paper and make the next cut.

9 Turn again and cut. Continue until the circle is complete.

10 Lift out the circle with the tip of your blade.

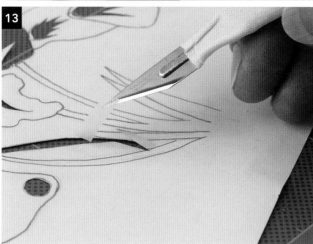

11 As you work, turn the paper over and hold it up to the light to see how the design is progressing.

12 If you need to repair a cut made in error, stick a piece of low-tack sticky tape to your cutting mat and cut out a small section. Lift it onto your scalpel.

13 You can now place the piece of tape wherever it is needed to repair the work.

Changing your scalpel blade

Change your scalpel blade regularly, as soon as the tip becomes dulled. This will vary according to the paper you are cutting, the way you hold the knife and the blade itself. To change the blade, first grip the old blade with jewellery pliers and pull it off. Pick up the new blade in the pliers and push it into place. This way, you don't use your fingers at all and the blade does not fly off the scalpel handle.

Iris

Here is the finished piece. I have cut this iris as a negative cut; removing all the leaf and petal pieces and leaving the flower shape in a black background. The template for this papercut is provided on page 136. There is also a template for a positive image of an iris on page 135.

Cutting with scissors

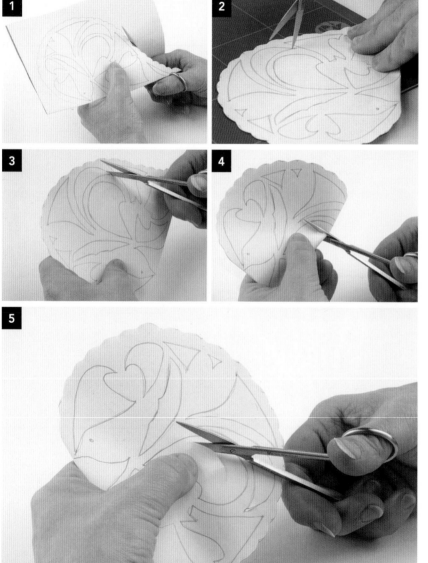

1 This is a folded papercut which will produce a symmetrical design. When drawing your design, make sure you keep the fold at the centre. Cut out the basic outline of the shape.

2 In order to make the first cut for the internal design, place the folded heart on your cutting mat and firmly jab the point of the scissors to make a hole.

3 Push the point of one scissor blade through the hole and begin cutting. Remove small sections gradually.

4 As an alternative to jabbing the scissor tips into the paper, you can make a soft fold and cut into it. This gives you a place in the paper in which to insert your scissor blade.

5 Cut out the rest of the design, ensuring that you only remove the negative areas of the design.

The finished papercut mounted on a black background for impact. This is a positive papercut where all the negative areas have been cut away.

Turning images into papercuts

Almost any image can be transformed into a papercut. The most successful papercuts will result from drawings you have done yourself based on your own sketches, ideas and imagination. However, if you are feeling nervous about drawing or want to start with something straightforward, try this approach first. Choose an image that naturally lends itself to pattern and structure in order to familiarise yourself with the process of seeing with a papercutter's eyes, identifying positive and negative parts and cutting patterns. A good place to begin is to use one of your own photographs of an object or shape that is graphic and linear, with a distinct outline.

Objects from nature are a brilliant way into this process. Beetles, butterflies, dragonflies, insects of all types, flowers and plants, trees, birds and feathers, fish and seashells are all sources of inspiration for me. In this instance, I found a seahorse given to me by my grandmother when I was a child. I like this because the seahorse's body is segmented into a clear pattern that will translate well into positive and negative cuts.

Note

At the outset of any papercut, you need to decide whether you are happy for the papercut to be the reverse of the image. If it is important to you that it is the same way around as the original image (as might be the case for faces in order to retain a likeness), trace the image, flip it over and then clip it to the carbon and cutting papers and follow the method shown opposite.

Transferring an image

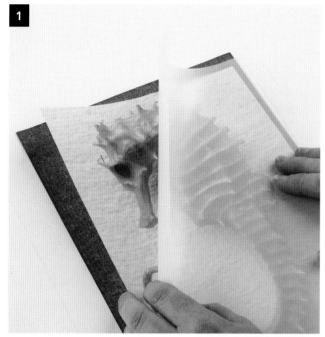

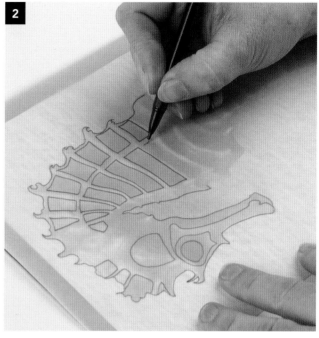

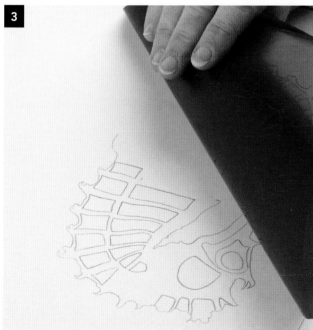

1 Layer the papers with the cutting paper at the bottom, white side up, then a sheet of carbon paper, shiny side down, then the image you wish to transfer, then tracing paper to protect the image. I usually use a black and white photograph as it helps to identify the contrasting tones, but I have used colour here for visual clarity.

2 Paper clip the papers along one side, then trace over the image so that the carbon paper transfers it onto the back of the cutting paper. Use a ballpoint pen or hard pencil. As you trace, try to envisage which areas will be positive i.e. left behind and which negative i.e. removed.

3 As you work, lift up the other papers to check your progress and to check that the image is transferring onto the back of the cutting paper.

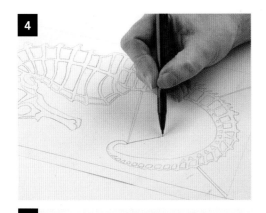

Creating a papercut

4 When the tracing is done, peel apart the papers to reveal the design. Now you can decide whether or not to add a border, and draw in anything you want to add to the design. I added a rectangular border and some lines to join it to the seahorse, because I wanted to make it look like a stained glass window.

5 At this point, take a long hard look at your drawing and decide which parts will be cut out and which will remain. You can mark the pieces to cut out or, if your brain works the other way, roughly shade in the areas you want to keep. If the image is of anything with a face, start with the eye. This seahorse has no white to the eye but with most faces, the white of the eye is a good place to start the papercut.

6 Cut out the design, starting at the centre and working gradually outwards.

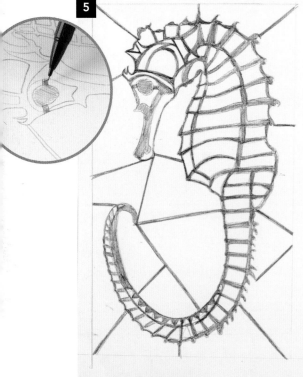

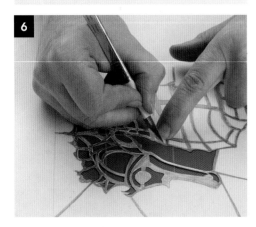

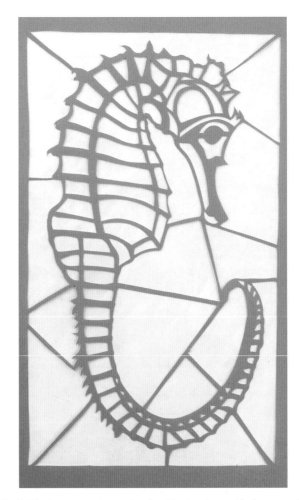

The finished papercut. A template for this piece is provided on page 132.

These are some other examples of the diverse images you can to turn into papercuts.

In this landscape, the student kept the horses in silhouette for emphasis and turned the fields into pattern .Author's own photographs.

The armour-like carapace of a grasshopper inspired this student's piece. Author's own photographs.

I transformed this photograph of my niece Zoë and her cat into this stylised portrait. Author's own photographs.

Art in Paper

Silhouettes

The earliest silhouettes or profiles appeared in England towards the end of the 17th century. The skills of the papercutter began to be deployed for figurative purposes, to capture likenesses. The process was less expensive and time-consuming than drawing a portrait. These images were known as 'shades', 'miniature cuttings', 'scissor types' or 'shadow pictures'.

Theories abound as to why they were eventually named after Etienne de Silhouette, the French Finance Minister under Louis XV. In keeping with the tradition of papercutting, the name may refer to the modesty and economy of the art form, because Etienne de Silhouette was known for his exceedingly mean fiscal policies. The connection to his name may also relate to his brief time in office, as 'silhouetting' was known to be a speedy process, like catching a fleeting shadow.

For the skilled silhouette artist, the scissor-cut drawing takes only a few minutes, but the skill may take a lifetime to perfect.

The 'something and nothing' quality of silhouettes appeals to me when I am designing a papercut. I love the solid 'something' of the silhouette standing out against the 'nothing' of the negative space around it.

Within my papercuts, I look to create a contrast between the solid silhouetted shape and the intricate patterns in the rest of the picture. In the Crow image above, the silhouetted tree shapes in the distance and leaves in the foreground stand out against the patterned crow. The silhouettes allow the eyes a moment to rest before they take in the whole of the cut image.

This study of a Morning Glory flower by a student in one of my workshops is, to me, utterly beautiful in its simplicity but also in its complexity. The student took the time to observe the flower carefully and then to do a detailed drawing before she cut it out. So while there is no escape into lyrical fantasy in this silhouette, it deftly conveys the nature and specificity of the flower through its delicate outline. Author's own photographs.

Red Silhouette

This silhouette, which I cut with a knife and not from life, was part of a sequence for a book illustration for a modern retelling of a fairy story. This picture represented one of the three murdered wives of the main character in the story. The silhouette neatly reflects the solidity of the once-living person alongside her shade – the essence of her soul. The blood red colour suggests her gory ending!

Stretch

We always think of silhouettes as being made up of solid colours. Stretch was one of a series of three images that were inspired by the movements of dancers. Each is cut from pages of Gray's Anatomy as I wanted the text and drawings of leg and arm muscles and bones to fill the silhouettes of the dancers.

Note

If you are considering cutting out the pages of a book, don't do as I did and cut the actual pages. It is a far better idea to photocopy the pages and then cut the photocopy. This is not because I have any strongly held aversion to cutting up books. I am mad about books, but their pages often become a palette for a collage or a source of materials for my workshops. Libraries sometimes give me their discarded books to cut up because otherwise the fate of that book is to be pulped. Instead I try to give old books a second life. The point here is that the book pages were incredibly thick and, inexperienced papercutter that I was at the time, the pressure of cutting them made my finger bleed.

Le Minuet

As an illustrator by training, I am always looking for ways to convey movement and depict story, which is how I came to create the silhouettes on this papier-mâché bust. It was made for an exhibition called The New Georgians at the Orleans House Gallery in Richmond, London. The idea was to celebrate the Georgian era in any material. I combined the 18th century craft techniques of gilding papier-mâché, curling or quilling paper and papercutting profile portraits of dancers on the fan headdress. The piece is called 'Le Minuet' after the lively dance that became so popular in Georgian times. This is a detail. To see the whole bust, go to page 128. Author's own photograph.

Chagford Hares

This very large papercut of the Chagford Hares – more than a metre (1 yard) square – took many weeks of planning and cutting. It was made for the Chagford Inn in Devon, UK. Chagford sits on the edge of Dartmoor and the image was designed to reflect aspects of Devon countryside – old gates, stone walls, plant life – as well as the birds of the region.

The three running hares are a local symbol and I knew from the outset that they should stand in silhouette to the rest of the cut image. This is because, even though the cutting is very intricate and detailed, it is difficult in a papercut to create a sense of distance or perspective. The near-silhouetted shapes of the hares (only their ears, noses and eyes are cut out) allow this symbol to stand proud of the rest of the image so that the hares appear to be in the foreground. Author's own photograph.

Portraits

I started my papercutting antics in the life-drawing studio, so I have always taken a great interest in learning to use my knife to draw the human face. My approach is, in many ways, a natural extension of silhouetting a face. Early silhouette artists began to add features and details to their work, embellishing with paint or ink. In my work, I love the stark, pared-down quality of a knife-cut drawing. You can create a great deal of expression with the angle of an eyebrow or the shape of a mouth.

When I am drawing a portrait for use in print or online, I always start with a cut-out of the character. I then refine it and colour it digitally. Remember that when cutting out a face, you must always reverse your drawing to retain the likeness to the individual. This is because the human face is asymmetrical and looks different if its features are swapped over!

Cutting a portrait

This is not a portrait of anyone in particular. It is a face I sketched and cut out in a workshop to demonstrate the technique of holding the features in place. Any resemblance to any person, living or dead, is purely coincidental!

1 Cut the portrait, leaving paper links or bridges supporting the various features and joining them to the rest of the design.

58

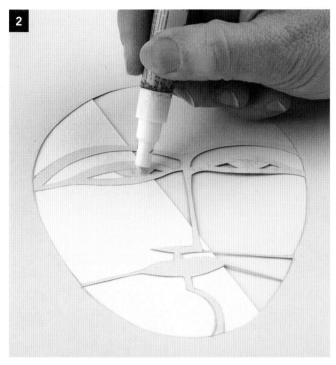

2 Apply glue pen to the back of any features that will be unsupported when you cut away the links. Also apply glue around the edge of the face.

3 Stick the papercut down on the background paper, applying gentle pressure to the features and other glued parts. Now you can cut away the supporting links from the front of the design. However, if you like them, you may want to keep the links and bridges to add another dimension to your papercut of a face.

The finished portrait.

Amy Johnson

This is my portrait of Amy Johnson, Britain's most famous aviatrix, who disappeared on a routine flight in 1941. It was based on a photograph and produced for a papercutting portrait workshop at the National Portrait Gallery, London. As you can see, all the facial features except for the eye on the right-hand side are connected to the outline of the face. I have cut away the paper links around the eye on the right. Her sheepskin collar, depicted as a pattern of jellybean-shaped negative cuts, frames her face. I have mounted the image on sky blue. Notice how the curve of the cut paper under her nose and lower lip suggest the contours of her face and a hint of shadow. Author's own photograph. The template for this papercut is provided on page 141.

Opposite
Queen Catherine

In this illustration of Queen Catherine Howard, fifth wife of King Henry VIII of England, I started with a basic black papercut, which I then scanned and transformed into a stained glass window. This is because I wanted to use jewel colours to describe the Queen's opulence. The stained glass window also gives the image a slight feel of the period despite the presence of an odd red-beaked bird. I have removed all the connecting lines in the Queen's face because I wanted to give it a simplified, glass-like texture and serenity. Author's own photograph.

Mark's Window

In this commissioned piece, the brief was to make a picture that would evoke Mark Conroy's life and passions, including his work as a London expert, tourist guide and television presenter. I needed a framework in which to bring elements as varied as Charles Dickens, St Paul's Cathedral and Alan Turing together in an illustrative way. Walking through Trafalgar Square in London, I spotted the window of St Martin-in-the-Fields. This contemporary church window offered me a wonderfully dynamic set of spaces within which to organise all the elements of the papercut. Author's own photograph.

This was also a portrait piece that was meant to be a strong likeness of Mark as opposed to a caricature or interpretation of his face. I worked from a photograph, carefully selecting the positive parts – the elements of his face that defined his character such as the slightly raised right side eyebrow, the shape of the beard and the tiny variations in the spacing of the teeth.

In a black and white papercut, there is inevitably much smoothing out of the features. You are unlikely to include every line and crinkle. The trick is to find the key personality elements.

You can also see that all the facial elements are still connected. This is partly because of the glasses but also because of the overall stylistic approach of the image. Author's own photograph.

Map of Samuel
This is a portrait of novelist and playwright, Samuel Beckett, based on a famous photograph. Having said you are unlikely to include every line on a face, in this case I was very taken with the network etched by age into Beckett's skin and made this papercut portrait as a study of ageing. Author's own photograph.

James

I was asked to design an album cover for The Reckoning by singer-songwriter and producer Ethan Johns. The songs were a collection of ballads and poems about two imaginary brothers, James and Thomas, who lived in Devon in the 1860s, then emigrated to the USA to live in northern California. I made a portrait of each brother for the inside of the cover. This is James.

I have included three stages of the image development process to show how I develop a drawing into a papercut drawing and then refine, redraw and colour it ready for printing.

The linking nature of a papercut was a useful design constraint, giving me a circular, contained shape within which to set the image. The visual elements around James give us clues to his character, history and – unsurprisingly perhaps with guns, gambling and passion in evidence – his likely fate! Author's own photograph.

Pete Postlethwaite

This was a book cover design for a biography of the late, highly acclaimed actor. It is an example of how I believe a papercut drawing can capture sensitivity and subtlety in a face. The process was as with other portraits: a black papercut which I then scanned and coloured with muted tones. Author's own photograph.

Michael Caine

The unmistakable actor. In this stylized image, prepared for a portrait-cutting workshop at the National Portrait Gallery, I wanted to make a cinematic-style cut drawing, showing how shadow can be conveyed in black paper. Author's own photograph.

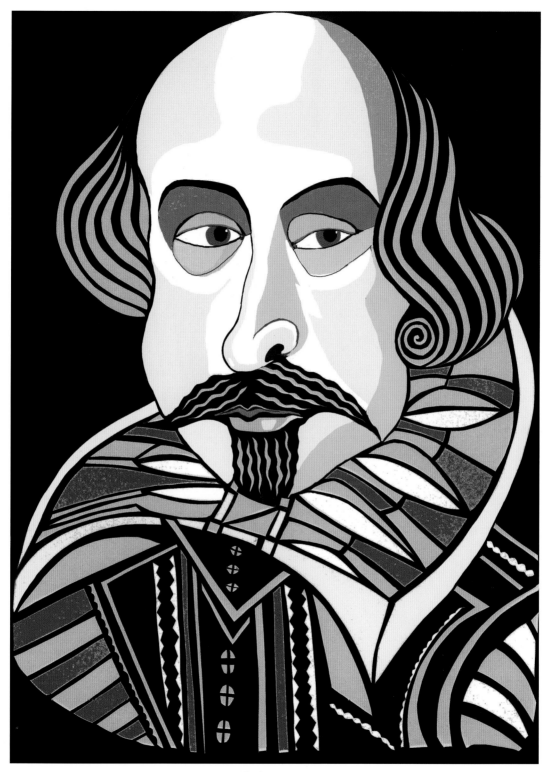

Shakespeare

Here I was playing with an iconic image of William Shakespeare, combining both my illustrator's and my papercutter's approach to make a humorous and memorable image. The collar and costume, which frame the face, gave me a rich pattern palette that I later digitally enhanced with tone and texture. Author's own photograph.

Landscapes and cityscapes

Landscapes and their urban equivalent, cityscapes, can reflect our emotional connection to a place. A landscape can be a dynamic backdrop to a person's life, whether it is a town or farmland, a wilderness or a tower-blocked skyline. In some papercut landscapes, I try to capture this sense of drama through the use of light and shadow. In others, I use the papercutting form to convey the story held or hidden in the landscape.

Deer in Richmond Park

How do you convey atmosphere and a sense of space in a landscape papercut? In this example of deer in Richmond Park, UK, the distant silhouettes of the trees are the positive areas of the paper. In the foreground, the other strongly positive objects are the upper bodies of the deer. I was fascinated by the interwoven grassy tapestry of the parkland and the camouflage it offers the deer as they melt into its structure.

Jane's Garden

Yacht

I was commissioned to make a seascape: a papercut to celebrate a long marriage, a love of sailing, Gibraltar and cats. The waves became the predominant pattern; their splash and currents exaggerated by the angle at which the yacht is tipping. Gibraltar is conjured via distant palm trees and two foreground dolphins. The cat is an improbable silhouette on the rails of the boat. Author's own photograph.

Opposite
Jane's Garden

I was asked to design a cover for a book about Jane's Garden. This image is the opposite in style to Deer in Richmond Park (previous page). This is a more classic papercut approach in which I have kept everything in the landscape in one dimension. It evolved from another papercut called This Land is Our Land. Both were destined for American homes. This highly stylised landscape describes a garden by the sea, populated by plants and birds of the region. Author's own photograph.

71

I am interested in experimenting with papercut drawings; layering and photographing them in different ways to vary the effects of light and shadow. There's more about this on pages 119–125.

I took this photograph on London's South Bank on a bright winter afternoon. I was attracted by the silhouetted tree shapes, the strong shadows and the sense of perspective enhanced by lines and posts receding into the distance.

I decided to divide the image into two layers. The top layer would literally be the objects that were either closer or more distinct. The bottom layer would be the parts of the image that were further away or more delicate – such as the mesh of bare branches.

I placed the two layers on perspex sheets (though glass would work equally well), held apart by books at either end. I then used a small spotlight to point the light into just left of the centre of the image. I moved the light around until I found a set of shadowy tones I liked.

The original photograph (author's own).

The papercut in progress. Author's own photograph.

The two layers of the papercut displayed on perspex sheets.

Winter Day on the South Bank
This is the final image, digitally unaltered. Author's own photograph.

Fashion

A magpie sits above these words and is a hint that I am a collector of beautiful antique images, because they can often be a brilliant starting point for a papercut. These fashion pages are my homage to some of the great fashion illustrators and photographers. I have borrowed some of the classic images to show how you might bring three different papercutting treatments to fashion subjects.

Opposite
Fashion Silhouette
I chose this picture – based on an old black and white fashion magazine photograph from the 1950s – for several reasons. First and foremost, the marvellous silhouette created by the hat, the gloved hand elegantly tipping it and the arched back pose. In the original photograph, the model is standing in front of a window. I chose to reduce the window frame to three thin lines, two vertical and one horizontal, both as a contrast to the solid contour of the dress and to connect the figure to the sturdy black border. Author's own photograph. The template for this papercut is shown on page 143.

Winter Fur

Another fashion image from the past receives a new look as a papercut design. Here the black papercut is mounted on a collage of papers attached to different parts of the cut-out. I used an origami paper, a silk paper and some gold and blue bookbinding paper, all collected magpie-like over many years. I used the papers to enhance the sense of luxury and to reflect the period portrayed. Notice how you can capture the softness of fur with tiny zigzag cuts.

Keep Trying On Different Faces

*This is my homage to illustrator Francois Berthoud and designer Jean-Paul Gaultier's
1986 collection, inspired in turn by Russian Constructivism. I have translated the
original linocut and watercolour images into a papercut of facial expressions.
This is the opposite of the simplicity of the 1950s photograph piece on page 75. Here
the detailed papercutting brings a layer of story and a new energy to the drawing.
What face will she be wearing today? Author's own photograph.*

Book covers

The contained frame of a book cover is the perfect location for a papercut design. These pages show how through various commissions, I have worked with historical detail, symbolism, story and iconic images to create original papercuts.

When the publisher, Orion, commissioned the cover shown opposite, the brief was for a design for a factual history book that would have the same eye-catching appeal as a fiction paperback. I needed to come up with a design that would grab the eye but also be true to the Roman era of Spartacus. The author checked my drawing for historical accuracy.

Opposite
The Spartacus War
*Spartacus needed body armour, bare flesh,
a tattoo and an epoch-appropriate helmet,
as well as a horse. The two-colour design has
immediacy and the title is built into the piece
so that the cover feels like one whole image.
Body armour is achieved through a series of
small circles and Spartacus's dragon tattoo
reaches across his chest. I cut out six different
helmets before choosing this one. Author's
own photograph.*

BARRY
STRAUSS

THE
SPARTACUS
WAR

Anne Boleyn

Jessica Palmer

Anne Boleyn

Reading about Anne Boleyn's time at the court of King Henry VIII of England originally inspired this cover design for a booklet about her. At the end of her short time as queen, Anne was the subject of gossip and rumour among her ladies in waiting and the members of the court. The crows buzz about her head and snakes and lizards hiss and move towards her neck. She fingers the pearls at her throat in anticipation of her end. This was a black papercut portrait that I coloured digitally. Author's own photograph.

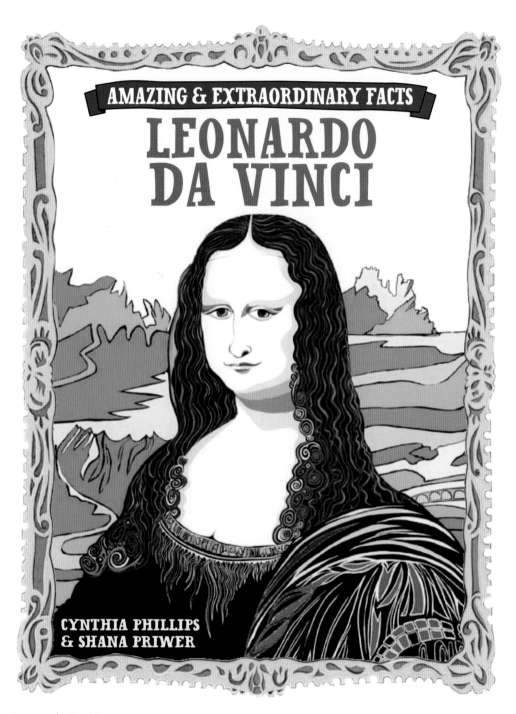

Leonardo Da Vinci

This was possibly one of the most challenging commissions I have so far received: to take the world's most iconic painting and make a papercut drawing of it for the cover of a children's book. In drawing the Mona Lisa in paper, I simplified many of the tonal aspects of the original painting into patterns; for example, the spirals in her hair and the folds of her drapery. It was essential to try to retain her expression, as this is one of the most significant features of the painting. The papercut frame and the limited colour palette enhance the focus on the details of face, clothing and hair. Author's own photograph.

Illustrations

It was during my Masters degree in Illustration that I first started to play around with papercutting. I had tried my hand at a variety of media, but I kept coming back to cutting and sticking. Although I now do a great deal of my work digitally, when I am looking for a way to illustrate text, a papercut design will often leap into my mind. The physical aspects of papercuts can often present ideas that support the content of a piece.

This image shown opposite illustrates an age-old folk song, learnt in a choir. The words instantly evoked this idea of the young birdcatcher with his birdcage open. He is effectively caged or trapped himself within the lower part of the papercut drawing, below the line that dissects the drawing horizontally. Meanwhile his unrequited love – in the form of the squire's daughter – gallops sidesaddle into the distance, unaware, pursued only by the freed birds.

Opposite
Love Without Hope
Author's own photograph.

Love without hope

As when the young
birdcatcher

Swept off his tall
hat

To the Squire's
own daughter

And let the
emprisoned
birds

Escape and fly

Circling about her
head as she rode by

Thomas Cromwell

Reading Hilary Mantel's book Wolf Hall made me want to do an illustration that would convey the claustrophobic pressure around this powerful figure.

I chose a fragment of text that I later discovered from Hilary Mantel had come from a poem by Thomas Wyatt. He was the last person Cromwell spoke to on earth. Hilary suggested to me that the deer pressing against Cromwell was like the contents of his unconscious mind. The cackling crows are the London lawyers, and they also represent Cromwell's enemies and friends. It is difficult to tell, though, which is which. The papercut form of closely connected elements lends itself well to the sense of a beleaguered man at the centre of a universe of intrigue.

The magazine for the city of Bath

THE BATH
magazine

www.thebathmagazine.co.uk

WHISPER IT TO ME

ISSUE 125 ♥ February 2013 ♥ £3.00 Where Sold

ISSN 2049-5447

Opposite and left

Whisper It To Me

In this image, I was keen that the figures within this fairytale-style evocation would seem to be emerging magically from the forest. The deer's antlers are branch-like. The figure's dress is part of the hedgerow. Plants spring from both creatures. I was looking to achieve an ethereal, whimsical quality. The image is about inspiration and the way in which ideas sometimes seem whispered into our ears when we are least expecting them.
The illustration was used on the cover of The Bath Magazine. They mounted it onto pale green and used two of my birds on top of the letters T and M, which helps link the image to the title. Opposite: author's own photograph. This page: reproduced with kind permission from The Bath Magazine.

She held back the swingi...
curtain of i...
and pushed back the...
opened slowly slowly

The Secret Garden

Frances Hodgson-Burnett's classic story was probably my favourite childhood book. I made this illustration for my website, to suggest a doorway into a world of imagery. For me, The Secret Garden is about unlocking our understanding of the wider world. It's a metaphor for the transition from childhood to adulthood. Perhaps it is also about wonder and openness. As a visual expression of the idea in the book, Mary is seen here emerging from a tangled thicket, pressing through the overgrown foliage and daring to open the door to the unknown but brightly lit world beyond the door.

The spirals, curves and twisted roots of the papercut followed naturally after I had the idea of peering through an opening – almost a keyhole – in the undergrowth. We see the door in the distance with Mary just reaching towards it. Her other hand holds back the springy branches. Her clothing is a series of lines crisscrossing with the strands of plant life. Within any illustration, I will always try to convey a sense of movement. I am trying to get the sense, in Mary's posture, that she is about to lean forward. The text is an integral part of this image and sweeps across the path like plant tendrils. Author's own photograph.

Charles Dickens on Marley's Ghost

This was less of an illustration and more the ghost of an idea for a poster for the Museum of London about events to celebrate the life of the author. I have included it here because I think the linear papercut style works well mounted on a copy of Dickens' manuscript for A Christmas Carol. Author's own photograph.

Mrs Simpson

In this image of Wallis Simpson, I was seeking to illustrate the character at the heart of the constitutional crisis of 1936 when King Edward VIII abdicated the throne of England to marry her. These events shook the establishment. The lion and the unicorn represent the United Kingdom. On the left of the image, Edward delivers his resignation speech. On the right-hand side, the new King and Queen await their turn.

I enhanced the angularity of the figure to create a caricature of Mrs Simpson as a stark and domineering presence. Author's own photograph.

Still life

What is a still life? To me it is a collection of objects placed together, which may be natural or manufactured. In this section, I have brought a range of differing papercut treatments to the traditional still life. I am drawn to movement and expression, so a still life is an unusual place for me to start, but the papercut form can introduce a dynamic aspect to an arrangement of inanimate items.

If I am designing a papercut still life, I don't necessarily look at these objects as three-dimensional. In fact, it makes a virtue of the medium to see the collection as a group of one-dimensional patterned objects. This was the thinking behind this collection of bird heads and feathers shown opposite. It was inspired by an entry from an old reference book about birds, showing types of feather and the birds from which they derived.

Opposite
Feathers
This papercut is in blue-grey for absolutely no other reason than I love the colour! Author's own photograph.

Ferns

This still life is similar to the Feathers image on the previous page; a collection of flattened-out natural objects. The papercutting is a simplification of their structure and form but no less beautiful for this. Author's own image. The template for this papercut is provided on page 137.

Garlic Bulbs

In this still life I have gone for the opposite treatment. I cut the design to look like a three-dimensional drawing and then embellished it digitally so that the solidity of the forms was emphasised.
The addition of black shadow increased the sense of the objects having solid form. The matt grey background exaggerates the shiny stripes of the garlic skins. Author's own photograph.

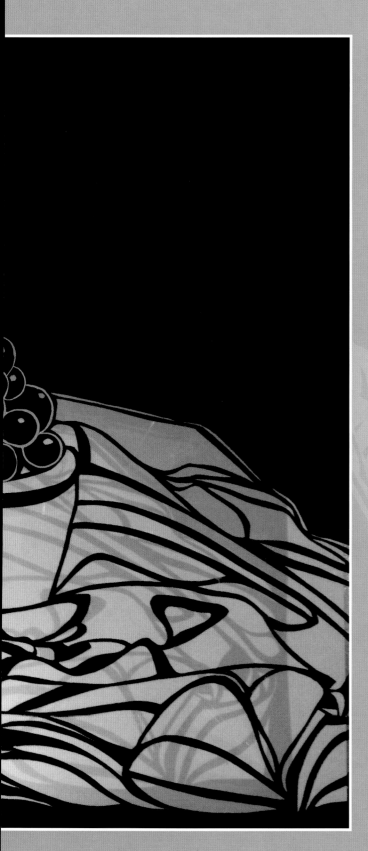

Black Still Life

In this still life, based on a classic arrangement of jug, bowl, knife, fruit and fabric, I first cut away the highlights from a sheet of black paper. I decided to make the sea of folds in the cloth the main feature of the piece. I then added the element of light by laying the image on glass and shining a light through it before I photographed it. The shadows of the pattern of the fabric folds add another dimension to the flat black image. Author's own photograph.

For more about using light with papercuts, see pages 118–125 on Shadow painting.

Animals

Animals are both kings and courtiers in my papercut drawings. In an illustration, an animal spirit, or animus, will help describe the subject of a portrait or what is happening in the story. Animals and birds dance around in my papercuts and give me opportunities for imagined conversations between the characters, for example Dance on pages 28–29.

Animal subjects allow you to draw the marvellous patterns in their fur, feathers, beaks, scales, shells and claws. There are superb contours in the shapes their bodies make as they leap, crawl, swoop and dive.

At other moments in my work, the animal itself takes centre stage, as in this depiction (opposite) of a tiger's face. It has a slightly cartoonish style but this is offset by texture derived from cutting the face from a watch advertisement in a magazine. I then coloured it digitally to accentuate the eyes and the colours of the fur.

*The template for the bird
papercut shown above is
provided on page 142.*

Tiger
Author's own photograph.

The Lunar Horse

This piece is about 1 metre (1 yard) wide by 60cm (23½in) wide. It was inspired by the Lunar New Year celebrations of 2014. It was the year of the horse, who is shown leaping into the garden of the New Year, attended by three joyful birds. Two of the birds are integrated, tattoo-like, into the pattern of the horse's flank. At the same time, the horse is kicking the dragon of the old year, 2013, off his back.

To make these large pieces, I usually start by sticking together several sheets of a paper to give me a large enough surface to cut out. Here I stained the paper red to reflect the oriental roots of the idea. Author's own photograph. A template for a simple Lunar Horse is provided on page 134.

Red and Green in Tooth and Claw

In this papercut I have concentrated on the contours of the animals' muscles and skin. This is an attempt to capture the lissome nature of black greyhounds; their elegant limbs and their nimble dexterity in pursuit of other creatures in the wild. The presence of a sea bass and two seagulls indicates that these two dogs live on the coast and love to run along the beach.
Author's own photograph.

Red Rooster

*Here the papercutting is focused on the pattern of the cockerel's feathers and comb, as well as
trying to encapsulate the sensation of sunrise in an old-fashioned, woodcut, story-book style.
The black papercut was mounted on textured paper, scanned and then coloured in sections.
Author's own photograph.*

The template for the bird image shown here is provided on page 140.

Using text

The fundamental questions about the relationship between papercutting and text are about relevance. It is essential that the text has meaning that relates to the image. It is also important that the text is in some way part of or embedded in the image as a whole. This all takes a fair amount of planning and if possible, you should always plan your design around the text. It is much more difficult to slot text in afterwards.

Text can be cut negatively, as in the clever image of Bob Dylan, shown opposite, by my student, Tim Whitton, who is also a graphic designer. Here the positives of the letters cascade around the singer's head, echoing the curls of his hair. Notice the way Tim has retained links or bridges so that he keeps the middle pieces of his letters.

Alternatively, text can be cut positively. In this case, the letters must link to each other to be held in place as you can see in the example below. A useful way to start positive papercut lettering is to write backwards in a generous, joined-up, cursive hand. There is an example of this on page 84.

All letters and words must be cut in reverse. To do this, it is very useful to have a reverse alphabet to hand, to help your mind adjust to the backwards thinking. It might seem hard at first but it's very good exercise for the brain!

Angelina Head
Portrait of Bob Dylan, by permission of Tim Whitton.

Here are three contrasting examples of text within papercutting.

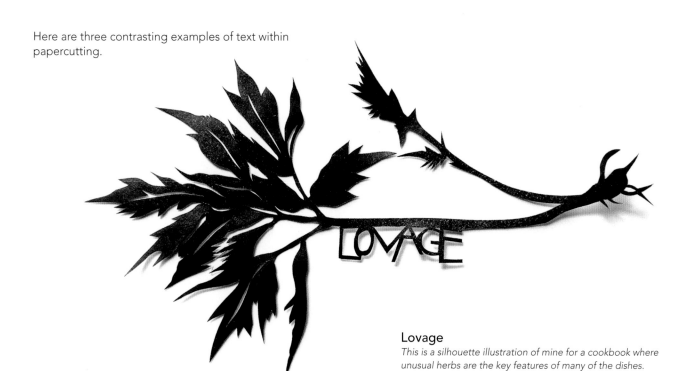

Lovage

This is a silhouette illustration of mine for a cookbook where unusual herbs are the key features of many of the dishes. As these herbs are unfamiliar to many people, the author wanted highly visible text to remind readers of the look and shape of these ingredients. Author's own photograph.

My Heart Pumps Blood Around My Body

This highly original piece was done by a student on a Valentine's day papercutting course at the Victoria & Albert Museum. While everyone around her was cutting out birds, bees and flowers, she took her own romantic route! I love the way the words curve around the lobes of the heart, emphasising its bulging shape; the blood-red colour of the paper and text; and the simplicity of the few fine cuts indicating veins. Author's own photograph.

106

Istanbul

This is a book cover design made by a student of mine, artist Bryony Miles. She cut the cover, based on a map of Istanbul and a silhouette of the city skyline, from four layers of paper. She cut the title out of the black silhouette in a negative font of her own design. The blue paper is silk paper that is threaded with silk and so conveys the feeling both of night sky and river water with its sparkly flecks. Author's own photograph.

Pleasure Garden Productions

I was asked to turn my 'Whisper It To Me' papercut into a company logo. This was one of the versions we experimented with as a possibility, turning the animal's mane into the text reading Pleasure Garden Productions. I like the way the text is an integral part of the image. Eventually, we chose much larger text so that it would still be legible when the logo was minimised, but I have included this as an example of a pretty way to use text in a papercut. Author's own photograph.

Put A Fork In It

This was inspired by a desire to show how silhouettes and pattern can be used to describe familiar objects in a beautiful way. I envisaged it as a header in a magazine article about antique forks. The text echoes the sharp, pointed fork shapes. The letters sit within horizontal lines, reflecting the sense of organisation on a carefully laid table. Author's own photograph.

Life drawing

Henri Matisse wrote: 'The paper cutouts allow me to draw with colour. For me, it is a simplification. Instead of drawing an outline and then filling in with colour – with one modifying the other – I draw directly in colour... It is not a starting point, it is a completion.'

It is no exaggeration to say that my life changed the day my life-drawing tutor, Jake Abrams, swapped my charcoal for scissors. In an instant, I was a convert to the joys of cutting and sticking. Since I started experimenting with using a scalpel to draw, I have found that my pencil drawing has improved immeasurably. Linear and contour drawing, which Paul Klee called 'taking the line for a walk', inspire me. When you draw with a knife, you commit to the linear outline in a very precise way. You don't dither around!

In my Drawing Life with a Knife workshops, we try out blind contour drawing: covering one eye to reduce awareness of three dimensions and looking only at the model, not the drawing. We then change to scissors instead of charcoal or pencil. Later we move onto using a scalpel, often working on the floor and drawing with a huge palette of coloured and recycled papers for texture, layers and emphasis.

Cutting out on the floor allows the student space to spread out her palette of papers and to use the knife on a firm, flat surface. Author's own photograph.

Opposite
You can use any mix of papers for drawing life with a knife. I am a particular fan of the way this student is trying out newspaper on black and white. Author's own photograph.

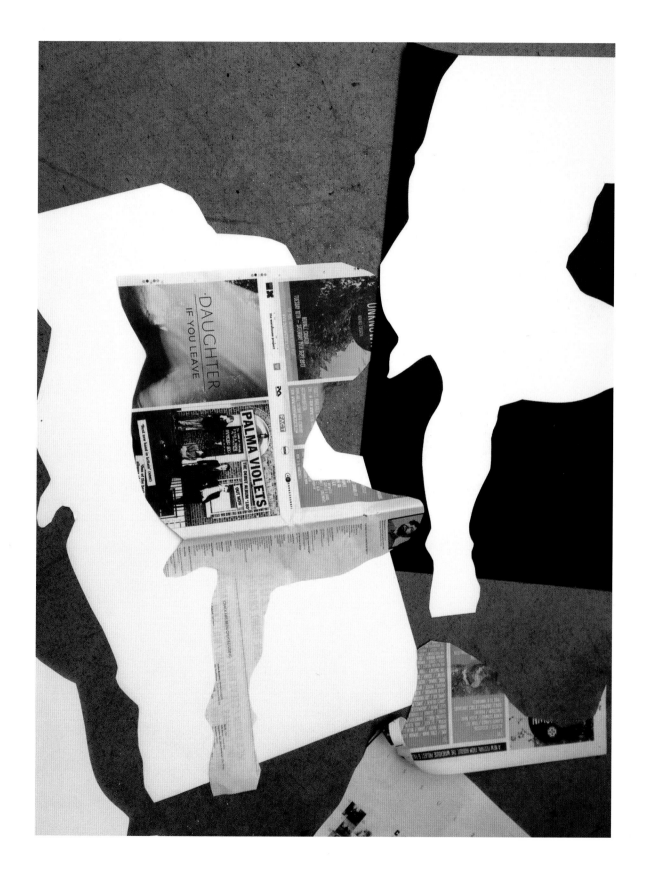

Life Drawing With Chair
Author's own photograph.

This drawing process encourages participants to see edges, lines, spaces, relationships, light and shadows, and to combine them as a whole. It can really help students who lack confidence in their drawing skills. It can also provide confident figurative artists with a fresh perspective on visually depicting the human form.

These are two examples from workshops where students have combined drawing in pencil with cutting out, either for emphasising a shadow (right) or simply for a playful design including the model's chair (above).

Pink Nude
Author's own photograph.

112

Two Figures

In this piece of, I have combined at least three techniques. I first drew the two figures by cutting them out. I then took a complex abstract pattern I had been cutting and stenciled through it with spray paint onto the two figures. I stuck the figures and the abstract pattern onto a sprayed yellow background. This was purely for fun. I like the end result because there is a sense of light shining through the abstract papercut onto the figures. Author's own photograph.

Pink Woman in Hat
This figure was cut freehand from several pieces by a student in a workshop. I love the choice of the recycled page from a magazine for the hat and the feeling of the unseen sun. Author's own photograph.

These are two poster-like examples in which there was little or no drawing with a pencil in advance. The one above is a student's work from a workshop and the one opposite is my own.

Opposite
Danger
Here I cut the woman's body from one piece of grey paper, partly sprayed with pale pink. Her head is only indicated on the second grey piece by the presence of lips. By introducing a word or piece of text, you not only provide contrast in the image, but you also create an opportunity to tell a story. Author's own photograph.

Clash of Identities

In this papercut I am again attempting to hint at a story. I originally cut the stylised figure of the kneeling woman out of two layers of newspaper. I then cut only the facial profile and outline from the second sheet. I arranged these on a piece of spray-painted paper. There is a lemon in the picture because the life model was holding a lemon at the time and for no other reason! Author's own photograph.

Seated Woman

I have included this image by a student as an example of negative figure cutting. The student took a sheet of grey paper and cut out the key areas she wanted to define. She then laid this single sheet of dark grey onto a sheet of yellow paper to create a simple yet striking drawing. Author's own photograph.

Shadow painting

Changing from scissors to a scalpel blade allowed for complexity and detail in my papercutting as well as fluidity and strength of line. But I also began to see that part of the beauty of papercuts is to see them as objects that can have a three-dimensional quality. Rather than always gluing images flat against a surface, I began to keep the curl of the paper for shadow and depth. Paper has substance. Henri Matisse is said to have enjoyed the flap and shiver of his paper cut-outs if a stray southern French breeze entered his studio.

I started to experiment with layering images on glass or perspex to add another dimension. I used a variety of light sources; applying a light from the back or below the image to exaggerate shape, texture and structure.

Opposite
Titania
This image is cut from green paper, layered on perspex and then black paper with a small torch shooting light in at the side. I am indebted to my friend, the portrait painter and designer, Richard Evans, for his photography. He helped me figure out this technique that I still use, for example in 'Winter Day on The South Bank' on page 73. Author's own photograph.

I may begin an image in pencil but the blade of the scalpel is what brings energy to the line and design. It leaves me with something fragile and flexible, and light can add theatricality and atmosphere. In these two images, *Once Upon A Time* and *Old King Cole*, I again experimented with lights and lamps of different hues.

Old King Cole

The figures here are framed in an exploding red book outline and mounted on glass over a white background. The shadows of the characters are visible on the white paper. Old King Cole teeters on his golden throne, expecting the court jester and his crew of birds and animals to entertain him. The jester waits warily to begin. He wears an audience of anxious faces on his body suit, and he is lit from behind as if on stage. The king's throne glows and adds to his majesty. His prodding finger extends as he demands, 'Amuse Me!' Author's own photograph.

Opposite
Once Upon A Time

This papercut sits above green tissue paper with a torch behind it, suggesting a mysterious night scene. Another torch catches the face of the sleeping girl and the beak of the crow as he leans over to tell the bedtime story. This dab of light adds a contour to the paper as if it is embossed, as well as a note of drama. Author's own photograph.

Peacock Parasol

Here are four images of the same parasol. In this piece, I was looking for new ways in which I might display a papercut in an exhibition – though these are working photographs taken in my studio. I cut this piece in two sections: the phoenix at the centre of the parasol and the crescent-shaped peacock on the outside. Tiny human figures, carrying parasols, leap from one giant bird to another in an effort to experience wingless flight.

Having fitted the papercut onto the skeleton of the parasol, I then photographed it with strong shadows. Why is it pink? Why not! In fact, I later recoloured it in blue and silver, and then mounted it in a box frame. Author's own photographs.

I Saw a Peacock With a Fiery Tail

This large shadow piece was inspired by the ancient, anonymous poem which begins: 'I saw a peacock with a fiery tail/ I saw a blazing comet drop down hail.' I have cut a number of peacocks, but this is the largest so far: 140 x 40cm (4ft 7in x 15¾in). It is cut from pure black paper and is suspended on a pink bamboo frame.

I cut this out with a view to lighting it but I had not realised what dramatic shadows it would throw up onto the wall. The image is lit from behind with a small clip-on light fixed to the frame. What I like about this treatment is that it enhances the stormy theme of the poem with the comet crashing down from the heavens, splashing and scattering the light. Author's own photographs.

Dragon

A student at the Victoria & Albert Museum cut out this little dragon, and we gave it the shadow treatment. We laid it on a sheet of thin perspex, suspended above white paper. The vertical lines are the patterns embedded in the perspex – an unexpected bonus, practically invisible to the human eye but picked out by strong light. Author's own photograph.

3D papercutting

For me, this means the process of developing a two-dimensional papercut into a three-dimensional shape. I am interested in the flexibility of cut paper, the manner in which the paper is changed by cutting into it and the possibilities of using this altered material in a variety of ways. The piece opposite is one of a series I made to explore the limits of what it is possible to do with cut paper. Often, as you will see in the rest of this chapter, I find myself making 3D objects from papier-mâché or layered paper, and then adding two-dimensional papercuts for decoration.

Opposite
Black Shoe
I first made the outline of the shoe, as a cobbler would from leather, and then I cut filigree patterns into it, and glued it into place on a sole and a heel made of paper. It was important that the cut filigree pattern was tightly formed, as looser cutting would have allowed the shoe to collapse. Author's own photograph.

White Bird of Paradise

For this image, I cut dozens and dozens of individual feathers from a huge variety of white papers and then stuck them in place layer by layer. Author's own photograph.

Le Minuet
This was one of a series of Georgian papier-mâché busts, made to commemorate the George I's accession to the British throne in 1714. As part of the New Georgians Exhibition at the Orleans House Gallery in Richmond, this bust was chosen to illustrate the Georgian craft passions of papier-mâché, paper quilling and curling and silhouetting. The silhouetted figures on the fan celebrate the energetic dance of the moment in the late 18th century – the minuet. Author's own photograph.

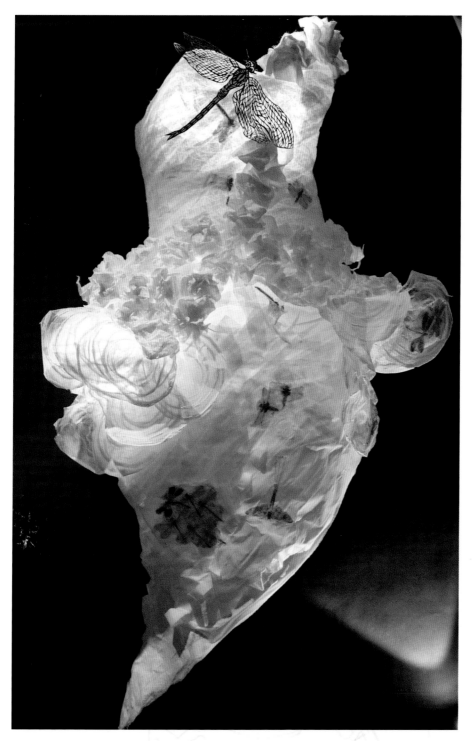

Dragonfly Dress
This dress was an experiment with light and a 3D paper object. I was seeking to illuminate the dress from the inside so that it would have an ephemeral, twilight feel, with a scattering of damselflies, spiral petals of paper and a large papercut dragonfly sitting like a decorative piece of jewellery or lace at the neckline. Author's own photograph.

Paper Tutu

This piece reflects my love of dance. It was made in a similar way to the Dragonfly Dress on the previous page, with layers of paper. The ruffle of the tutu is made with crumpled paper that was then cut and folded into white leaf shapes. The bustier of the dress is moulded from dress pattern paper. The wisps at the neckline and leaves on the shirt are cut from a high-quality, extremely expensive art newspaper! I suspended the piece from the ceiling with nylon thread in an exhibition and it twirled gently in the air. It now lives with a close associate of the UK's Royal Ballet School. Author's own photograph.

Tudor Paper Galleon

The Tudor House Museum in Southampton approached me to make this Tudor paper galleon to link with *The First Cut* exhibition in Sea City Museum. Every part of the galleon, including ropes, sails, hull, masts and mermaid, is made from paper. Both the ship and the mermaid are created from many layers of paper over a paper frame. The hull of the ship is made primarily of Tarasen grass paper using traditional papier-mâché techniques. The Tudor House is famous in historical circles for its Stuart Ship Graffiti that is engraved into the walls of one of the rooms of this ancient house. The graffiti is of sailors, dancing figures, animals, bird and ships. I turned the graffiti into delicate papercuts to decorate the sails and hull. All are cut from black paper except for one that is cut from black and gold check paper. I also cut Tudor roses and used cut paper stars and strips of contrasting paper to emphasise portholes and other features of the ship. Paper birds sit on top of the masts and a mermaid carries the ship on her back, home to the safety of the harbour. She also carries a paper shell and amphora found on the seabed, echoing objects held in the museum collection. Author's own photograph.

131

You can trace or photocopy these templates to transfer onto your own paper for cutting. If you scan them, you can resize them as required. The templates are of gradually increasing complexity. Remember that some are positive papercuts and others are negative – where the background colour remains. They are all in black and white but you can cut them out of any colour or even patterned paper.

This template is for the Seahorse papercut shown on pages 46–48.

This template is for the Lunar Sheep papercut on pages 10–11.

This template is for a simple Lunar Horse. A more complex version is shown on pages 100–101.

This template shows a positive image of an iris, as referred to on page 27.

This template is for the negative image of an iris shown on page 43.

This template is for the Fern papercut shown on page 94.

This template is for the Seed Head papercut shown on page 26.

This template is for the Ash Tree papercut shown on page 37.

This template is for the chapter heading papercut shown on page 104.

This is the template for the Amy Johnson portrait shown on page 60.

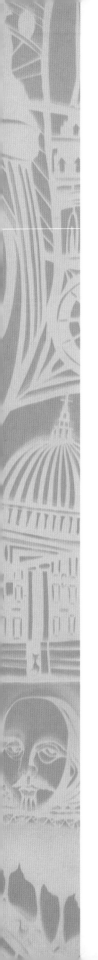

This template is for the chapter heading papercut on page 98.

This is the template for the Fashion Silhouette papercut on page 75.

Index

THE CANADIAN ROCKIES

LAND OF THE SHINING MOUNTAINS

ALBERTA COLOR

ABOUT THIS BOOK

This impressive collection of superb photography portrays the unique natural beauty and rich diversity of the Canadian Rockies, or the "Land of the Shining Mountains", as they were known to early aboriginal people. Images from this wonderful landscape are presented with brief informative text and selected quotations.

OTHER TITLES FROM ALBERTA COLOR

Alberta Beauty, a Portrait of the Province
Rocky Mountain Majesty, Images of the Canadian Rockies
Picture Perfect Edmonton
Jasper Treasures, Beauty in the Canadian Rockies
Canada's Rocky Mountains

FRONT COVER
Mount Assiniboine Provincial Park

DESIGN, EDITORIAL & PHOTOGRAPHY
Ron & Noreen Kelly, Alberta Color
Additional Photography
  • Richard Wear, pages 74, 74-75, 76-77, 78
  • Brian Wolitski, pages 40, 57, 70-71

Revisit the beauty of Canada at our website www.beautyseen.com

PUBLISHED & DISTRIBUTED BY
Alberta Color
4149 98 Street
Edmonton, Alberta
Canada T6E 5N5

MADE IN CANADA

Take a Peek

3

"GIVE ME THE ISLANDS OF THE UPPER AIR.
ALL MOUNTAINS,
AND THE TOWERING MOUNTAIN TREES."

Hilda Doolittle, American poet (1886-1961)

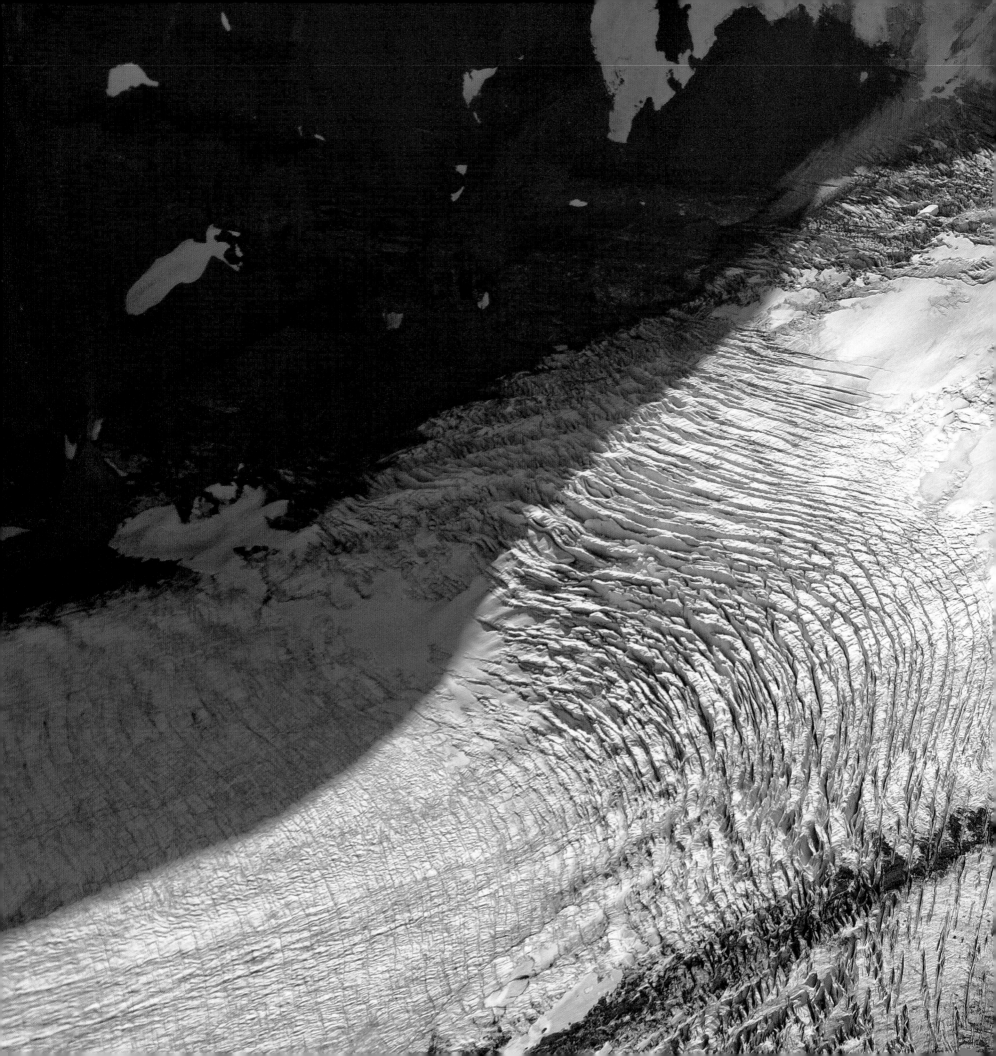

How Cold

RIVERS OF ANCIENT ICE

✽ ✽ ✽ ✽ ✽ ✽

GLACIERS ARE REALLY FROZEN STREAMS OF COMPRESSED SNOW & ICE, CREEPING DOWN MOUNTAIN SLOPES, WEARING AWAY VALLEY WALLS AND CARRYING ERODED ROCK DEBRIS TO LOWER ELEVATIONS. A MAJOR FORCE IN THE EVER-CHANGING LANDSCAPE, THE GLACIERS OF THE CANADIAN ROCKIES ARE AN IMPORTANT SOURCE OF FRESH WATER FOR MUCH OF WESTERN NORTH AMERICA.

COLUMBIA ICEFIELD

Jasper National Park

Brittle surface ice cracks as it is stretched over uneven bedrock at the base of the glacier, resulting in deep, dangerous splits, or crevasses, *above*.

The thick ice mass of the Columbia Icefield lies on a wide, elevated plateau, surrounded by some of the highest peaks in the Canadian Rockies. Tremendous pressure turns accumulating snow into ice, forcing a way through gaps in the mountains and forming great frozen tongues, *left*. Dense glacial ice contains no light-dispersing air bubbles and reflects the blue end of the visible spectrum, creating the characteristic turquoise color.

9

ATHABASCA GLACIER

Jasper National Park

Specialized snow coaches, *above*, travel a constantly shifting road to the surface of the glacier, where in places the ice is estimated to be 305 m (1,000 ft.) thick.

A series of three icefalls, or steps, can be easily seen at the headwall of Athabasca Glacier, *right*, the most accessible glacier descending from the massive Columbia Icefield. One of six main "toes" of the Icefield, the glacier moves at a rate of several centimeters a day.

PARKWAY
ICEFIELD
Jasper National Park

The Icefield Parkway passes through the heart of the Canadian Rockies tracing the Continental Divide from Banff to Jasper. A highlight of the 230 km (143 mi.) journey is a stop at the accessible and fascinating Athabasca Glacier.

Dazzling Drive

NAMED FOR THE MANY SPECTACULAR ICEFIELDS AND GLACIERS THAT FLANK IT, THE ICEFIELD PARKWAY IS JUSTIFIABLY DESCRIBED AS ONE OF THE MOST BEAUTIFUL DRIVES IN THE WORLD. IN RECOGNITION OF ITS UNIQUE GEOLOGICAL VALUE AND STRIKING NATURAL FEATURES, UNESCO DESIGNATED IT A WORLD HERITAGE SITE IN 1984.

❋ ❋ ❋ ❋ ❋ ❋ ❋

SASKATCHEWAN GLACIER

Banff National Park

Female "nanny" mountain goats, *above*, form nursery groups to protect and nurture their young. Although sometimes competitive when defending their space, they spend most of their time grazing on grasses, twigs and leaves.

The Saskatchewan Glacier, *left*, curves down from the eastern rim of the Columbia Icefield. The primary water source for the North Saskatchewan river, it is one of the longest glaciers in the Rockies, with a length of 13 km (8 mi.).

Early morning sun highlights Dome Glacier, visible behind the environmentally-friendly Icefield Centre, *right*. The facility offers opportunities to learn about the icy mysteries of the glaciers.

The Columbia Glacier, *left*, descends from the northwest edge of the Columbia Icefield. Meltwaters at its toe are the source of the mighty Athabasca River.

How High

ROCKS THAT TOUCH THE SKY

◆ ◆ ◆ ◆ ◆ ◆ ◆

THE SPECTACULAR PEAKS OF THE CANADIAN ROCKIES CONTAIN QUARTZITE, LIMESTONE AND DOLOMITE, ALL HARD ROCKS WITH HIGH EROSION RESISTANCE. MANY MOUNTAINS IN THESE RANGES RISE OVER 3,352 M (11,000 FT.). THE HIGHEST OF ALL IS MOUNT ROBSON, WITH AN ELEVATION OF 3,954 M (12,973 FT.).

CASTLE MOUNTAIN

Banff National Park

Huge, distinctive ears give mule deer, *above*, their name. Preferring "edge" habitats where trees meet grass, these bounding animals can often be seen beside the road.

Gently sloped layers of rock alternate with near vertical cliffs to create the distinguishing "castel- lated" profile of Castle Mountain, *left*, rising beside the Bow River along the Icefield Parkway.

MOUNT
RUNDLE
Banff National Park

Looming over the edge of Banff town-site, the flat, slanting slabs of rock that form the western face of Mount Rundle make it an easily recognized peak. The Vermilion Lakes provide a perfect mirror for the mountain.

"MOUNT RUNDLE IS MY BREAD AND BUTTER MOUNTAIN. I NEVER TIRE OF PAINTING IT, FOR IT IS NEVER THE SAME. ITS COLOUR RUNS THE GAMUT FROM ORANGE TO COOL BLUE-GREY, WITH OVERTONES OF VIOLET AND INTERVALS OF GREEN."

Walter Phillips, Canadian watercolour painter (1884-1963)

CASCADE MOUNTAIN

Banff National Park

The Sulphur Mountain Gondola, *above*, carries visitors up the mountain to enjoy a panoramic view of the Bow River Valley. The discovery of hot mineral springs on the lower slopes of Sulphur Mountain led to the establishment of Banff National Park in 1885.

Cascade Mountain, *left*, a significant peak near the Banff townsite, dominates the scene from the summit ridge of Sulphur Mountain. Tunnel Mountain and the famous Banff Springs Hotel are also visible from this vantage point.

MOUNT EDITH CAVELL

Jasper National Park

Large ground squirrels known as hoary marmots, *above*, live on mountain slopes near the treeline. Their high-pitched warning call has earned them the nickname, "the whistler".

In his *Description of and Guide to Jasper Park*, visiting celebrity Arthur Conan Doyle admiringly described Mount Edith Cavell, *left*, "Almost due south of Jasper, this massive snow-crowned mountain rises high above the surrounding peaks, its white summit glistening in the sunlight." The famous author visited the park in 1914.

Emperor of the Rockies

"OH, WHAT A GLORIOUS SIGHT! WITH HIS HIGH FLUNG CREST MANTLED WITH A THOUSAND AGES OF SNOW, MOUNT ROBSON SHOULDERED HIS WAY INTO THE ETERNAL SOLITUDES THOUSANDS OF FEET HIGHER THAN THE SURROUNDING MOUNTAINS."

George Kinney, an early climber on Mount Robson (1872-1961)

Often caused by weakened layers of snow, a sudden, dangerous slide down a mountainside becomes an avalanche. Avalanches leave trails of buried and broken trees, rocks and other debris in their wake, *left*.

The golden light of sunrise highlights the rich colour and texture of the rocky, snow-dusted peak of Mount Wilson, *right*, near Saskatchewan River Crossing.

PYRAMID MOUNTAIN

Jasper National Park

The Jasper Tramway, *above*, provides opportunities for panoramic views of Mount Tekarra, as well as other Jasper landmarks.

Beautiful Pyramid Mountain, *left*, stands north of Jasper townsite. The gentle contours and reddish, oxidized iron hues are typical of many peaks in the Victoria Cross Range, a group of mountains in Jasper Park honouring recipients of the Victoria Cross.

MOUNT ATHABASCA

Jasper National Park

Warm summer days release the exposed ice at the toe of the glacier, *above*, allowing the new-born water to rejoin its ancient cycle.

Almost entirely above the treeline, the snowy, glacier-covered peak of Mount Athabasca, *left*, rises to a height of 3,491 m (11,454 ft.). Easily accessible from the Icefield Parkway, this mountain is a popular choice for climbers, whose tracks can be seen in the snow.

How Vivid
Colour Beyond Belief

~~~~~~~~~~~~~~~~

Oh, the amazing colour! Where does it come from? The brilliant lakes in the Canadian Rockies are sparkling pools of clear water set in bowls of mountainous rock lying at the feet of glaciers. Minute particles of ground rock suspended in the water reflect the blue-green part of the spectrum, creating the rich, incredible hues.

PEYTO LAKE

Banff National Park

Golden yellow cinquefoil blooms, *above*, can survive below freezing temperatures. Also known as potentilla, this hardy deciduous shrub can grow at an elevation of 3,500 m (11,500 ft.) in the Rocky Mountains.

From the air, the silty delta created by the melting ice of Peyto Glacier at the south end of Peyto Lake is easy to see. Mount Patterson is the impressive peak on the right.

UPPER WATERTON LAKE

Waterton Lakes National Park

Distinguishing features of black bears, *above*, include round ears, small eyes and a tapered nose with a straight facial profile.

Waterton Lakes National Park, where rugged mountain peaks rise steeply from the eastern grassland plain, is part of what is sometimes known as the "Crown of the Continent". The southern shore of Upper Waterton Lake, *right*, crosses into the United States as part of Waterton-Glacier International Peace Park.

MALIGNE LAKE

Jasper National Park

Chipmunks, *above*, are small squirrels commonly seen in mountain environments. They scurry everywhere, constantly searching for seeds, nuts, insects, grain and birds' eggs that make up the bulk of their diet.

The largest natural lake in the Canadian Rockies, beautiful Maligne Lake, *left*, is ringed with snowy glacier-topped peaks. Cruiseboats allow visitors access to the lake's most famous view, serene Spirit Island, part way down the 22 km (13 mi.) long lake.

LAKE LOUISE
Banff National Park

Lake Louise is a beautiful natural area that is home to a wide diversity of recreational opportunities, including outstanding hiking.

Named for a Princess

LAKE LOUISE WAS KNOWN AS "HO-RUN-NUM-NAY" OR "LAKE OF THE LITTLE FISHES" TO THE STONEY FIRST NATIONS PEOPLE. IN 1884, IT WAS GIVEN ITS PRESENT WORLD-FAMOUS NAME IN HONOUR OF PRINCESS CAROLINE ALBERTA LOUISE, DAUGHTER OF ENGLAND'S QUEEN VICTORIA.

The aquamarine palette of Lac Beauvert, *left*, and nearby lakes provides a stunning setting for Jasper Park Lodge and its famous golf course.

Brilliant turquoise water of Banff's Moraine Lake, *right*, dazzles through the lakeshore trees.

47

BOW LAKE

Banff National Park

In springtime a young moose, *above*, splashes hurriedly through recently melted icy water.

Impressive Crowfoot Mountain and the cool, translucent water of Bow Lake, *right*, rank high among the many treasures that border the Icefield Parkway. This glacier-fed lake is the source of the Bow River; its water eventually flows into the Atlantic Ocean.

MORAINE LAKE

Banff National Park

Dense, brightly coloured bracts of pretty Indian paintbrush, *above*, add splashes of red and orange to the forest floor.

The Valley of the Ten Peaks provides a stunning backdrop for the exquisite blue of Moraine Lake, *left*, creating one of the most famous views in the Canadian Rockies.

On the steep slopes of Mount Robson, Berg Glacier, *right*, kisses the surface of teal blue Berg Lake . Pieces of ice often "calve" off the glacier and fall into the water.

Melting ice from Bow Glacier and the Wapta Icefield, *left*, fills a rocky bowl with turquoise water until it overflows and runs into Bow Lake.

How Fast

Water In A Hurry

It starts as a Trickle from its icy mountain source, gradually gathering volume as it spills over rocky ledges, crashes through steep canyons or meanders along wide river valleys. All the water in the Canadian Rockies eventually flows into one of three oceans: the Pacific, the Atlantic or the Arctic.

ATHABASCA RIVER

Jasper National Park

During the fall, the distinctive bugling call of the bull elk, *above*, sounds throughout the valleys. The impressive antlers, sometimes used in aggressive wrestling with other males to establish dominance, grow new and are shed every year.

Major fur trading routes along the Athabasca River and its valley, *left*, played a significant role in the history and settlement of the Canadian West. The river's path through Jasper varies from narrow gorges with swiftly rushing water to alluvial flats braided with wide channels. The 168 km (104 mi.) section within Jasper National Park is part of the Canadian Heritage Rivers System.

ATHABASCA FALLS

Jasper National Park

The common dipper, *above*, named for its curtsying habit when perched, hunts for food by diving into swirling white water.

Glacier-fed Athabasca River, *right*, carries huge volumes of tumbling water over a hard quartzite ledge at Athabasca Falls, south of Jasper town on the Icefield Parkway. The falls cut into the softer underlying rock layers, creating potholes and other intricate features.

Thundering Takakkaw Falls, *left*, in Yoho National Park exhibits the classic characteristics of a hanging valley waterfall.

A series of suspended walkways and bridges provide pathways to experience the cool depths and beauty of Johnston Canyon, *right*, west of Banff. This limestone canyon contains seven waterfalls and plunges 30 m (98 ft.) at its deepest point.

BOW RIVER

Banff National Park

The massive spiraling horns of the male Rocky Mountain bighorn sheep, *above*, form a tight curl close to the face. Head-butting crashes in dominance battles with other males often cause blunting at the tips.

The Bow River, *right*, flows east towards the prairies past Banff, the famous mountain town nestled in the valley at the foot of mighty Mount Rundle. Reeds growing along the river banks were historically used by local First Nations people to make bows and are the river's namesake.

NORTH SASKATCHEWAN RIVER

Banff National Park

The North Saskatchewan River begins life at the foot of the Saskatchewan Glacier in the Columbia Icefield. The Icefield Parkway intersects the river at The Crossing, where many channels create a braided stream flowing across the valley floor.

Water on a Journey

"WHY HURRY, LITTLE RIVER,
WHY HURRY TO THE SEA?
THERE IS NOTHING THERE TO DO
BUT TO SINK INTO THE BLUE
AND ALL FORGOTTEN BE."

from "The River" by Frederick George Scott (1861-1944)

MALIGNE CANYON

Jasper National Park

The humid environment at the floor of Maligne Canyon supports unexpectedly lush plant life. A willow sapling, *above*, takes root in the silt-filled crack of a large rock surrounded by swirling water.

Churning water crashes through Maligne Canyon, *right*, creating a narrow limestone chasm more than 50 m (165 ft.) deep in places. Several bridges cross the dramatic gorge, allowing dizzying views of rocky walls, mossy ledges and the thundering Maligne River.

Beside the Icefield Parkway, the beautiful cascades of Tangle Falls, *right*, spill dramatically down the steep slope during spring runoff.

Torrents of silty meltwater from the Columbia Icefield pour over Sunwapta Falls, *left*, south of Jasper. Shortly below the falls, the Sunwapta River joins the Athabasca.

How Wild

PARADISE DWELLERS

What a thrill to catch a glimpse of a wild animal in its natural setting! The mountains and valleys of the Rockies provide ideal habitat and protection for large mammals like bears, wolves, elk and moose, as well as a refuge for many birds, fish and rodents.

BIGHORN SHEEP

The distinctive horns of the bighorn ram, *above*, continue to grow throughout the animal's lifetime, and may reach a weight of over 13 kg (28 lb.) in a full-grown male.

Gregarious Rocky Mountain bighorn sheep, *left*, typically gather in groups of 8 to 10 individuals; bachelor flocks of male rams usually stay apart from female ewes and their young.

BEARS

Recognizable by their distinctive concave facial profile, shoulder hump and large claws, grizzlies, *above*, range the entire mountain landscape from burnt forest floors rich in new growth to river flats where they hunt for spawning fish. Rising onto their hind legs is a sign of curiosity, not aggression.

Typically shy, black bears, *right*, are primarily forest creatures, preferring the protection and vegetation of dense bush and wooded areas.

Call of the Wild

"FOR THE STRENGTH OF THE PACK
IS THE WOLF, AND THE STRENGTH
OF THE WOLF IS THE PACK."

Rudyard Kipling, novelist (1865-1936)

Highly adaptable and intelligent, wolves live together in groups consisting of an alpha pair of unrelated adults and their recent off-spring. These close-knit packs hunt together and can travel long distances in search of prey. Hunting skills are often practised and improved by play behavior.

Solitary and territorial, cougars, or mountain lions, *left*, avoid human contact whenever possible. Their large feet and long tails make them fast, graceful runners and fantastic jumpers.

The impressive adaptability of coyotes, *right*, allows them to survive and even thrive in many habitats. Both curious and timid, they can be recognized by their long pointed noses and ears and their thick bushy tails.

ELK

Fresh snow clings to deciduous bushes, coniferous trees and exposed rocks along the Maligne River, *above*, creating a magical vista.

A diet of grass, leaves, bushes and saplings supports the white-rumped elk, the second largest member of the deer family. Insulated from the winter cold by their thickened coats, females live in groups or harems defended by dominant males.

"HOW GLORIOUS A GREETING THE
SUN GIVES THE MOUNTAINS."

John Muir, conservationist and founder of The Sierra Club (1838-1914)

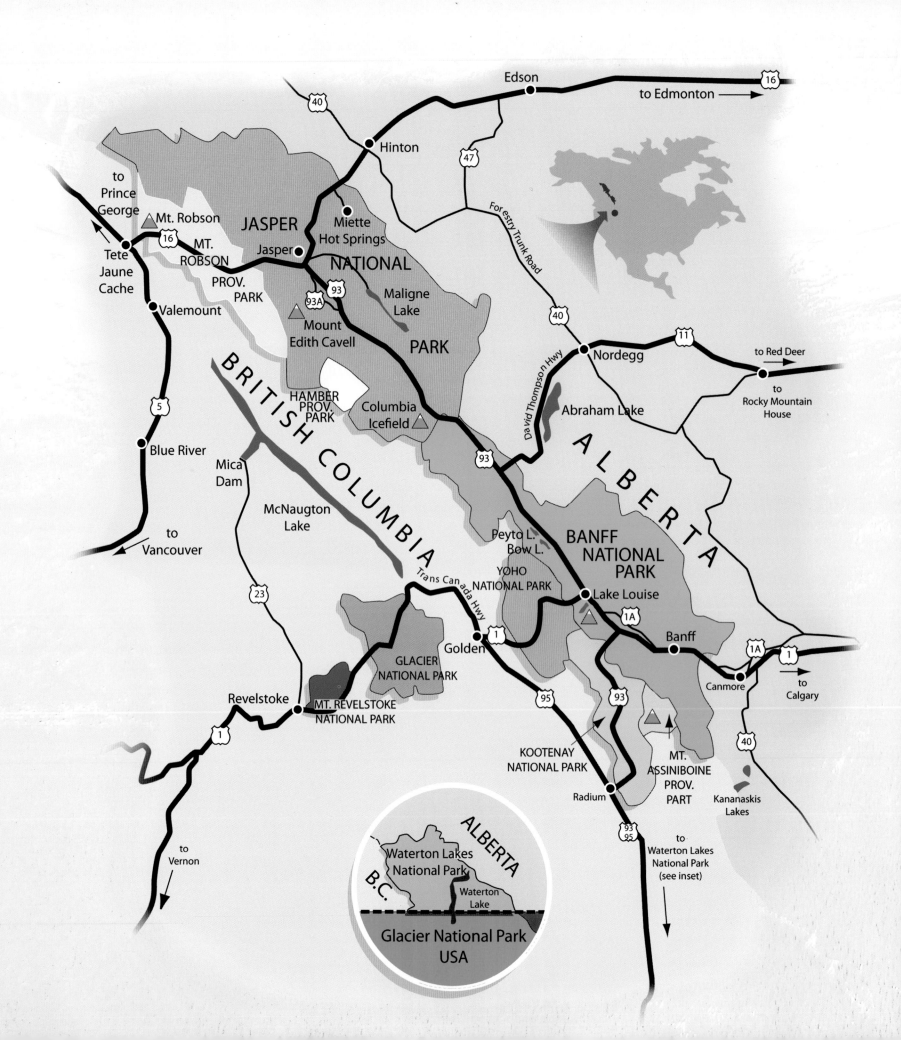

to Prince George

Mt. Robson

Tete Jaune Cache

16

MT. ROBSON PROV. PARK

Valemount

5

Blue River

Mica Dam

McNaugton Lake

23

Revelstoke

1

to Vernon

BRITISH COLUMBIA

JASPER

Jasper

93

93A

Mount Edith Cavell

HAMBER PROV. PARK

Columbia Icefield

Miette Hot Springs

NATIONAL

Maligne Lake

PARK

40

Edson

to Edmonton

16

Hinton

47

Forestry Trunk Road

David Thompson Hwy

Nordegg

40

11

to Red Deer

to Rocky Mountain House

Abraham Lake

ALBERTA

93

Peyto L.
Bow L.

YOHO NATIONAL PARK

Trans Canada Hwy

Golden

1

95

GLACIER NATIONAL PARK

MT. REVELSTOKE NATIONAL PARK

KOOTENAY NATIONAL PARK

Radium

93
95

BANFF NATIONAL PARK

Lake Louise

1A

Banff

1A

Canmore

1

to Calgary

40

MT. ASSINIBOINE PROV. PART

Kananaskis Lakes

to Waterton Lakes National Park (see inset)

ALBERTA

B.C.

Waterton Lakes National Park

Waterton Lake

Glacier National Park
USA

84